FOUL DEEDS & SUSPICIOUS DEATHS IN SUFFOLK

Foul Deeds and Suspicious Deaths in
SUFFOLK

Mark Mower

Series Editor
Brian Elliott

Wharncliffe Books

First published in Great Britain in 2008 by
Wharncliffe Books
an imprint of
Pen & Sword Books Ltd
47 Church Street
Barnsley
South Yorkshire
S70 2AS

ISBN: 978 184563 055 3

A CIP catalogue record for this book is available from
the British Library.

Typeset in Plantin and ITC Benguiat by
Mousemat Design Limited

Printed and bound in Great Britain by CPI UK

Pen & Sword Books Ltd incorporates the imprints of
Pen & Sword Aviation, Pen & Sword Maritime,
Pen & Sword Military, Wharncliffe Local History,
Pen and Sword Select, Pen and Sword Military Classics
and Leo Cooper.

For a complete list of Pen & Sword titles please contact
PEN & SWORD BOOKS LIMITED
47 Church Street, Barnsley, South Yorkshire,
S70 2AS, England
E-mail: enquiries@pen-and-sword.co.uk
Website: www.pen-and-sword.co.uk

Contents

Acknowledgements

A number of people have helped me in researching and writing this book, and I would like to express my thanks to the following for their kind assistance and support: Rupert Harding; Christine Mower; the staff of the Suffolk Record Office; and, most importantly, my wife Jacqueline for her tireless proofreading.

Introduction

The English historian Edward Gibbon once wrote that 'History is indeed little more than the register of the crimes, follies and misfortunes of mankind.' If that is the case, this volume presents a fair slice of history from the county of Suffolk.

Much is often made of Suffolk's agricultural heritage and the impact of this on the social, economic and environmental conditions of its many towns and villages. In 1841, over 40 per cent of the local population was employed in the cultivation of land, compared to an already declining 20 per cent in the rest of England and Wales. And while this proportion would decline in the hundred years that followed, Suffolk, like Norfolk and Cambridgeshire, would retain a disproportionate share of the nation's agricultural workforce.

The predominantly agricultural nature of the county helped to shape both its urban and rural environments and added much colour to the particular customs and practices of the people who lived there. But it also created a stark backdrop to the lives of many ordinary people. Rural poverty manifested itself all too often in inadequate housing, poor sanitation and appalling working conditions, and the seasonal, unskilled and weather-dependent nature of much agricultural work helped to keep wages low. Permanent and guaranteed incomes were uncommon for all but the burgeoning class of skilled workers employed in the newly emerging trades of the Industrial Revolution.

Poverty in Suffolk, as elsewhere, led to poor health, starvation, disease, alcoholism and early death. The average life expectancy of agricultural workers was only thirty-eight years and infant mortality was not uncommon. In 1863, there were 7,670 deaths in the county – some 37 per cent of these were of children under the age of 5.

Crucially, poverty also led to crime, and all of the tales featured in the book mirror the social conditions and attitudes created by the insular and rural nature of the county – from stories of highway robbery, smuggling and poaching, to accounts of appalling child cruelty. Some reflect the narrow-mindedness shown to outsiders and those with mental health problems, which could often prompt suicide or murder. Yet more are crimes of passion, fuelled by jealousy, drink or despair. And some simply reflect the criminal preoccupations of their time – from body-snatching to arsenic poisoning.

The ability of the criminal justice system to detect, investigate and prosecute criminals for their misdemeanours is a constant feature of this book. The local police force in 1864 amounted to fewer than 300 officers, and the number of crimes recorded in that year stood at only 272. While the number of officers would grow exponentially in the years beyond that, so too would the number and range of crimes they were required to investigate. Many of the cases in this book illustrate the growing professionalism and capabilities of the police in solving difficult crimes and the increasing reliance on forensic and medical science to secure convictions.

It is fascinating to reflect on the prevailing social attitudes, in an era before mass media, towards many of these foul deeds and suspicious deaths. Our modern-day interest in crime, suicide and murder is nothing new. Nineteenth-century newspaper reports covered significant deaths and murders in all their gory details. Public executions drew vast crowds of onlookers who often watched such events with a carnival-like enthusiasm. And widely talked about murders, like those of Maria Marten and Rose Harsent, created an insatiable demand for printed media. But it would be wrong to assume that this reflected only a prurient fascination with crime and death. Many people were willing to challenge the inhumanity of capital punishment, and large-scale petitions for the reprieve of condemned prisoners were not uncommon. Others campaigned for improvements in the social and economic conditions that gave rise to so much of the crime which blighted their communities. Where it has been possible, this book has sought to reflect both the popular and changing public attitudes to crime and death.

CHAPTER 1

The Case of the Black Dragoon
(1750)

'I never before desired a power of executing the legal penalties,
but if I had such a power I would exercise it in this case.'

When Tobias Gill first arrived in the village of Blythburgh in the summer of 1750, he could hardly have imagined that this sleepy, out of the way, coastal haven would become his final resting place. Not that he had any real say in the matter. For his untimely demise was every bit as unexpected as the death of the young woman he was convicted of murdering – a bizarre chain of events that led the well-travelled dragoon to the taut end of a hangman's noose and a tale that has become well established in Suffolk folklore.

Blythburgh itself is a small village in north-east Suffolk, just under a hundred miles from London and some four miles from the North Sea at Southwold. It is set in a landscape of outstanding natural beauty with a tidal river and a diversity of arable pastures, heath, woodland and marshes. The area itself is well known for its impressive medieval church, which sits on the main trunk road that links London and Great Yarmouth.

In the 1750s there were only twenty-one private homes and a population of around 125 people in Blythburgh. Much of the social and cultural life of the village was centred on public houses like the *White Hart*. Transport consisted of two wagons from London each week and one sailing vessel. In addition to this, the Great Yarmouth mail coach passed through the village every day, at ten o'clock in the morning and six o'clock in the evening, en route to London. The village was also an area of considerable commercial activity, including milling, shoe-making, farming, tailoring and blacksmithing.

Not all this commercial activity was within the law, however, and it was the ever-present and lucrative trade of smuggling that first brought the coastal communities of east Suffolk to the attention of the Revenue and Customs men. The illicit trade in goods from the Low Countries was endemic at this time, with smugglers bringing in tea, lace, silk, tobacco and bottles of spirit to avoid the heavy customs duties imposed on such goods. It was estimated in 1743, for example, that as much as half the tea drunk in Britain had been imported illegally as a result of coastal smuggling.

The local waterways provided accessible routes for the smuggled goods to be moved inland, and the River Blyth was particularly well used. A window of the *White Hart* was used to signal the 'all clear' to local boats which ferried their illegal cargoes across the marshes. At one stage, even the pews and altar of the medieval church were used to conceal the contraband.

The White Hart, *Blythburgh, which once had a special window that was used to signal the 'all clear' to local smugglers who ferried their illegal cargoes across the marshes.*

As early as the 1730s, the Customs Commissioners had drawn the Treasury's attention to the excessive smuggling taking place in Suffolk and the inability of their officers to stem the tide of this unlawful activity. As a result, companies of dragoons were drafted in from outside East Anglia to assist in patrolling the coastline. And so it was that a detachment of the 4th Regiment of Light Dragoons found itself based in the Blythburgh area from the summer of 1750. Some of these soldiers were billeted in local hostelries like the *White Hart*, unaware, perhaps, of how close they really were to the heart of the smuggling trade.

One of the dragoons billeted in Blythburgh was Tobias Gill, or 'Black Toby' as he was known to his fellow soldiers. Like the others, he had earlier seen service fighting in the Battle of Dettingen, in the War of the Austrian Succession, under the leadership of Colonel Sir Robert Rich. At over six feet tall, with a broad, muscular frame, and wearing his scarlet coat and waistcoat and green regimental breeches, the Black dragoon must have cut quite a dash. Perhaps it was no surprise that he became a favourite of many local women and the focus of much village gossip.

It was not unusual to find a Black soldier serving in the dragoons in 1750. Black slaves and free men had been recruited to serve in the British Army and to protect colonial interests as early as 1662. The Black recruits of the 4th Dragoons were mainly foot soldiers, although a few became sergeants and corporals. Some, like Gill, who served as a regimental drummer, were part of the musical corps.

These men were treated no better or worse than other soldiers. In fact, for all serving recruits at this time, life could be harsh. Conditions were poor; the food was generally bad and medical treatment was basic.

In comparison with their posting overseas, the dragoons must have viewed their initial arrival in Suffolk with some glee. Promised a period of rest and renewal, the soldiers were quick to take advantage of the hospitality offered by the local alehouses and very soon acquired a reputation for hard drinking, ill-discipline and brawling. Unpopular with many locals, who remained sympathetic to, if not tightly allied with, the smugglers, the hostility towards the dragoons began to grow.

And throughout the summer of 1750 the local press reported a number of incidences of petty crime and rowdiness in the area.

For his part, Toby Gill did little to help the growing unease of the locals. When sober, he was described as easy-going and charming, particularly when in female company. But after a few drinks he could become easily irritated and wildly aggressive, picking fights as a result of throwaway comments or the casual looks of those around him. Gill's fellow soldiers knew to keep out of his way and very soon he was banned from drinking in Blythburgh and forced, instead, to seek ale and company in other nearby villages.

One evening in June 1750, while returning from one such drinking bout, Gill met Ann Blakemore, a local barmaid from Walberswick, on the road across the heath about one mile west of Blythburgh. The popular account of what followed is that Ann recognized the dragoon and, realizing he was heavily drunk, tried to hurry past him. Being annoyed that she would not speak to him, Gill is then said to have pursued the girl, catching her by the loose ends of her neckerchief. Folklore has it that he then raped and murdered her before collapsing in a drunken stupor beside her.

The actual nature of the events that night may never be known. What is clear is that Ann's dead body was discovered on the heath the next morning by three labourers, as they made their way to work. Beside her lay Toby Gill, still drunk and unconscious.

The village constable was called for and Gill was taken into custody. He could remember nothing of the night before. On Monday, 22 June a coroner's inquest was convened at short notice. The case against Gill was purely circumstantial and informed mainly by the accusations of a number of local residents. Gill admitted being drunk on the night in question, but emphatically denied either raping or murdering Ann. The coroner acknowledged that no marks had been found on Ann's body and there were no obvious signs of any struggle – no evidence, in fact, to suggest either rape or murder. Despite this, Toby Gill was found guilty of both crimes by the inquest and committed to Ipswich Gaol.

In his trial at the Bury St Edmunds Assizes in August 1750, Gill continued to protest his innocence, but was found guilty of both crimes. He was described as a 'drunken and profligate fellow', and in summing up the trial judge played to the popular sentiment of the time by declaring, 'I never before desired a power of executing the legal penalties, but if I had such a power I would exercise it in this case.' The dragoon was sentenced to be hung in chains near the spot where Ann's body had been found.

On Friday, 14 September 1750, Toby Gill was transported from Ipswich Gaol to face execution. The event had been well publicized. An advertisement in the *Ipswich Journal* on 5 September declared:

> *Whereas it was thought that Tobias Gill, the Black Drummer, who was condemn'd at Bury Assizes for the murder of Ann Blakmore, would be executed at Ipswich; this is to inform the publick, that he will certainly be executed at this town, on Friday the 14th instant, and afterwards will be hung in chains near the place where he committed the act. He will be brought from Ipswich Gaol to the Angel in this town on Thursday the 13th instant.*

Even the choice of Friday, as market day, was designed to ensure that the event drew the largest possible crowd. As it turned out, the execution would take place not in Bury St Edmunds, but at the four crossways in Blythburgh – a clear example of local 'justice' being seen to be done.

Gill continued to be vocal in declaring his innocence and pleading for his life when faced with the gallows. At the sight of the ten o'clock mail coach, he made a desperate plea to be given a chance to save his life, offering to have a halter put around his neck and a rope tied to the end of the coach, so that he could try to outrun the carriage and four horses. But the reply was a swift and definite 'No'.

Having been hanged by the neck until dead, Gill's body was placed on a gibbet and left to swing in chains. Here it remained for some months, until the weather and wildlife on the heath had removed the flesh from the bones – a singularly repugnant chastisement that was reserved for the very worst of criminals and remained in use officially until 1832. Gill's remains were eventually interred by his soldier colleagues in the churchyard of Blythburgh's Holy Trinity Church.

The churchyard of Holy Trinity Church in Blythburgh, where Toby Gill's remains were eventually interred by his soldier colleagues.

Very little is known about the unfortunate Ann Blakemore. History has failed to record even the most basic details of her life. By comparison, Gill's infamy was to live on for many years. The gibbet in Blythburgh was allowed to stand for fifty years before falling to pieces. It is claimed that the nails from the structure were made into a thatching comb by a local roofer.

In an ironic twist of fate, it was the local smugglers who did most to preserve the memory of Toby Gill. Inventing numerous ghost tales about 'Black Toby' and the headless driver of a mail coach being drawn by four headless black horses, the smugglers sought to keep people off the local heathland and indoors at night as they plied their illicit trade along the highways and waterways of north-east Suffolk. To this day, the area close to the crossroads, where the A12 meets the old path over Blythburgh Common, is known locally as 'Toby's Walks' in recognition of these supernatural tales.

The legend of the Black dragoon was also immortalized in an epic poem of twenty-seven verses in Ernest Read Cooper's *A Suffolk Coast Garland*. This contains the memorable lines:

An' if aat midnight time yaou staan',
Just ware them gallers stood,
Fooks saay yaou'll hare a carriage come
A rattlin' down o' the rood;

Fower hosses blaack without no hids,
A Fun-ril hus behind,
A blaack man settin' on the box
A drivin' loike the wind;

They saay 'cos Toby hain't no graave,
Noor yet no parsin bell,
He're got ter come hare iv'ry night,
An' drive hisself ter hell.

Judged by modern standards, it is hard to see the case of Tobias Gill as anything other than a gross miscarriage of justice. In the face of the available medical evidence, and principally on the basis of unsubstantiated opinion, it seems as if the Black dragoon was tried and convicted more as a result of village tittle-tattle than any discernable or reliable evidence. As such, his execution for the rape and murder of Ann Blakemore in that summer of 1750 remains an appalling, if enduring, tale of rough justice.

A signpost for 'Toby's Walks', a recreational area in Blythburgh where Tobias Gill was hanged.

CHAPTER 2

Terror on the Highway

(1783)

*Brandishing a pair of horse pistols, Steggles cried
'Damn you! Your money or your life!'*

Highway robbery was a persistent threat to travellers since the dawn of history. From the seventeenth century it became so prevalent in England that William Fennor observed in his 1617 book *The Counter's Commonwealth*, that 'Newmarket Heath and Royston Downs . . . [are] . . . so full of highwaymen that poor country people cannot pass quietly to their cottages'. Much is made of the exploits of infamous robbers like Richard 'Dick' Turpin, but Suffolk too had its share of thieves and vagabonds who preyed on the unfortunate along the highways and byways of the county. And while the authorities struggled to bring but a fraction of these felons to book, some did come within the full purview of the law.

One of the earliest recorded highwaymen operating in Suffolk was the celebrated Reverend William Cratfield, the de-frocked rector of Wortham, near Diss. Legend has it that this seventeenth-century clergyman became a career criminal, robbing travellers on Newmarket Heath alongside another villain called Thomas Tepyrtone. His colourful activities were thought to include not just highway robbery, but extorting protection money from other felons. In an illustrious career that is said to have lasted over ten years, Cratfield is portrayed as ending his days incarcerated in Newgate Prison, where he eventually died. More recently, it has been suggested that Sid James's highwayman character in the film *Carry on Dick* was based partly on Cratfield's supposed exploits.

The reality behind the story of the highwayman vicar is no less fascinating than the folklore that has built up around him. But the popular accounts of his criminality are a good 200 years out in placing him in Suffolk during the seventeenth century. In fact, a William Baret de Cratfield did exist and at one time was indeed the rector of Wortham. He came to Wortham in the last decade of the reign of Henry IV and began as the rector of the parish on 12 July 1401, replacing the previous incumbent, Johannes Cockerel de Eye, who had been in the position for some fifty-two years.

Wortham Church, where William Cratfield, the highwayman vicar, was once rector.

Initially enjoying the patronage of both his parish and the abbey of Bury St Edmunds, the troubled clergyman lasted only seven years as rector, before disappearing one day to resurface some time later as a cut-throat and thief on the roads around Newmarket. He had taken to a life of crime alongside an accomplice called Tepyrtone (or Typertone), who was a failed hosier from London.

Records contained in the *Calendar of Letter-Books of the City of London*, show that Cratfield and Tepyrtone were the subject of an inquisition held at Newgate on 28 September 1416. The entry reads: 'The said jurors further find that William Cratfield, late rector of the church of Wortham . . . and Thomas Tepyrtone, late of London, "hosyer," did, on the 28th May [1416], rob William Boton[er] of London, "goldsmith", of a sum of money, and that they are notorious highway robbers and murderers.'

The record of the inquisition ends with the proclamation that sheriffs are to 'take the aforesaid William Cratfield and Thomas Tepyrtone if found within their bailiwick' and goes on to say, 'They disappear, however, and after being called at five separate Hustings are outlawed according to custom'. This was indeed a blow for the pair, as the earlier writs issued against them were only valid within the district of London in which the crime had occurred. By leaving the area the two men had effectively avoided the sheriff and his men. But being declared 'on exigent' they became outlaws who could now be hanged without as much as a hearing.

There seems to be some uncertainty about what happened to the errant highwayman in the years that followed. Some accounts suggest that he met a young woman and fell in love – a romance that eventually led to his death. A law report in 1418 apparently declared that 'A parson of Wortham . . . who has haunted Newmarket Heath for some time, robbing and despoiling many of the King's subjects, was now with his concubine brought into Newgate where lastly he died.' However, this seems to be a premature account of his demise, for the *Calendar of Letter-Books* lists the eventual indictment of Cratfield and Tepyrtone for 'divers felonies' in 1432. It seems likely that both men would have faced the hangman's noose in Newgate for their misdemeanours.

Many other criminals were to follow William Cratfield's lead in terrorizing the roads of East Anglia. Thomas Rumbold was hanged at Tyburn on 27 October 1689 for his life of robbery, deception and cheating in Suffolk and Essex. His partner in crime had been Margaret Matthews, the daughter of a sword-maker from Lavenham. She had died a year earlier, having retired on her ill-gotten gains.

Dick Turpin himself made occasional forays into Suffolk, the rich pickings from travellers to the Newmarket racetrack making the county an attractive proposition. Old coaching inns, like the *Bell Inn* in Kennett, claim to have been regular stopping-off points for Turpin and other highwaymen, although records

The Bell Inn *at Kennett, a coaching inn reputed to have been a regular stop-off point for highwaymen like Dick Turpin.*

supporting this are scarce. What is well recorded is Turpin's ride from London to Bungay in the winter of 1737. Along with his colleague, Tom King, the highwayman robbed two ladies who were collecting £14 for corn. King was unwilling to rob the pair, saying it was a pity to take money from such pretty girls, but Turpin persisted and relieved the ladies of their hard-earned cash.

No less scandalous were the exploits of highway robbers James Wilson and Thomas Kersey. Operating on the roads between Bury St Edmunds and Brandon, Wilson would dress as a gamekeeper and lure unsuspecting travellers towards him. When they were within range he would level his shotgun at the unfortunate victims and demand their belongings while Kersey would emerge from his hiding place to collect their valuables. Apprehended for robbing a Mr Parker of Thornham, the men were tried at the Bury St Edmunds Assizes on Monday, 17 March 1760. Wilson, undoubtedly the cleverer of the two, struck a plea-bargain with the court and escaped execution, while Kersey was hanged on 12 April that year.

While some proved to be highly accomplished in their dubious activities, it would be wrong to assume that anything more than a handful of highway criminals was successful in evading the law for long. And as the cases of Walker and Steggles showed very clearly, it was not always the victim that paid the heaviest price.

Walker was an opportunistic highwayman, who was drawn into a life of crime in order to fund his other nefarious activities. On Sunday, 12 January 1777, he attempted to rob the Norwich stagecoach, one and a half miles outside Newmarket on the road to Barton Mills. He was armed with only an iron candlestick, but managed to stop the coach. Unfortunately for him, one of the passengers took exception to the highwayman's approach and shot at him. Walker dug his spurs into his horse and attempted to make off, but rode only a few yards before falling to the ground. He was picked up and carried to the *Red Lion Inn* in Newmarket where he died an hour later. It transpired that the 23-year-old had inherited a considerable fortune some years before and had led a depraved life in London before taking up his later illicit profession. He died leaving a wife and children in the city.

James Steggles was no more fortunate when, acting on a tip-off, he attempted to rob a man in the village of Barrow near Bury St Edmunds on the evening of Monday, 6 January 1783. Steggles, a blacksmith and petty criminal originally from the nearby village of Tuddenham, waylaid wealthy farmer William Macro as the latter was walking home from the *Red Lion* public house where he had been collecting a considerable sum of tithe money. Mounted on a borrowed brown horse and wearing a waggoner's frock (see the advertisement on page 133), bob-wig and handkerchief to cover his face, Steggles pulled up to the farmer close to Barrow Hall where Macro lived. Brandishing a pair of horse pistols, Steggles cried 'Damn you! Your money or your life!' Seemingly unfazed by the gun pointing at him, Macro struck out at Steggles with his walking stick, but missed the highwayman's arm. Steggles fired the pistol at point blank range, but failed to hit his target. The lead slug grazed Macro's cheek and singed the shoulder of his frock-coat but left him otherwise intact. Stunned that his victim was not wounded, Steggles pulled the horse around and took off at great speed across an open field, having failed to discharge the second of his two pistols. Not content with his lucky escape, Macro tried to run after Steggles with cries of 'Stop thief!' before making for home, still in possession of his tithe money.

William Macro's subsequent actions served only to confirm that James Steggles had indeed picked on the wrong person to rob that night. Up early the next morning, Macro walked back to the scene of the crime and followed the distinctive hoof prints for five miles across the fields and as far as *The Bull* public house in Kentford. Here he discovered a brown mare in the

A private home in Kentford, once The Bull *public house where James Steggles was apprehended by William Macro.*

stable and a shocked Steggles in the kitchen of the inn. Having been apprehended, Steggles was committed to Bury St Edmunds Prison pending further inquiries.

Macro did not let the matter rest there, however. When taken at *The Bull*, Steggles did not have with him any pistols or his highwayman's disguise. Macro was eager to find the garb in order to secure the conviction of his assailant. Having learnt that the highwayman's brother, William Steggles, lived in Barrow and was suspected of being the person who had tipped off the highwayman about the tithe money, Macro knew he had a valuable lead. On the morning of Thursday, 16 January, a neighbour informed Macro that William Steggles had set off towards Kentford. Macro lost no time in riding at speed along some back roads to get to the Kentford *Bull*. Having correctly guessed that the brother had been making for the inn, Macro hid in a room next to the kitchen to see what he was up to. William Steggles stopped to pick up James Steggles's boot stockings, spurs and whip, before informing the landlord, William Norman, that he was going on to Newmarket, some five miles away.

Still eager to continue in his quest, Macro waited until William Steggles was out of sight then remounted his horse, passed over the brook at the back of the inn and took the Moulton Road to Newmarket. As a skilled horseman with an excellent knowledge of the geography of the area, William Macro again outwitted his quarry and arrived in Newmarket ahead of Steggles. He arranged for a man to watch out for the horseman's arrival and to observe his movements. He was later told that Steggles had stabled his animal and had taken a fresh hack-horse from the *Half Moon* inn on the High Street, intent on riding to the *Black Bear* in Cambridge. Not to be outdone, Macro called on a friend in Newmarket and having explained his mission, asked if Mr Eaton would ride with him to Cambridge to gather any further intelligence they could.

Both men rode to Market Passage in Cambridge where the yard of the *Black Bear* coaching inn was located (now the site of the Guildhall). On inquiry, Eaton learnt that William Steggles had travelled to Cambridge to collect some clothes from his brother's lodgings in the city and to let the landlord of the *Black Bear* know that the brown mare he had lent his brother some ten days earlier was now at the Kentford *Bull*. Steggles had also said to the landlord that he would not let the authorities know whose horse it was as he feared it might cause further trouble.

When William Steggles had set off once more towards Newmarket, Eaton and Macro made further inquiries about James Steggles, the highwayman. They learnt that he had worked for the previous six months with John Jeffries, a tin worker in Cambridge. However, Steggles had been detained only a couple of weeks before at the gaol on Castle Hill, on strong suspicion of stealing forty guineas from the home of Mr Haley, a baker in the city.

Armed with this new information William Macro returned to Barrow, tired but invigorated. The next morning he began his searches again and re-traced the route of Steggles's getaway on the night of the shooting. At one point the route crossed a ditch, and perceiving that the rider had stopped at this point, Macro searched the thick bushes nearby. Under some very long grass, he was delighted to find the highwayman's wig. Knowing that the other items were likely to be hidden close by, the ever-industrious farmer arranged for the bushes to be cut in the days that followed and on Monday, 20 January he was rewarded with the discovery of the brace of horse pistols, the handkerchief and some iron shot.

In the run-up to Steggles's trial, there were other events locally that illustrated just how unsafe the highways of Suffolk had become. On Monday, 3 February 1783, a stagecoach from Stowmarket was stopped by two armed highwaymen. They robbed one of the passengers inside and stole two parcels from the coach. Not content with this, they then threatened to kill two farmers who happened to be passing at the time. Later that month, on Saturday, 15 February, Samuel Roberts and Nathaniel Lilley were brought by *habeas corpus* from Newgate Prison to Bury St Edmunds Prison, where Steggles was still being held, to face trial for robbing a Mr Whittle on the highway near Sudbury, Suffolk.

The following day, there were astonishing scenes at the gaol. Samuel Oxer and Joseph Everard, who had been convicted of breaking into the shop of Thomas Hawes, the Mayor of Sudbury, and stealing various goods in January, tried to escape, along with Samuel Roberts and another prisoner. Oxer and

Everard managed to break out of their cells and drop down into the yard of the prison but were apprehended by the gaoler. Oxer later confessed that as part of the escape, the men had planned to murder the turnkey and gaoler.

James Steggles faced trial at the Bury St Edmunds Assizes in March 1783. During the proceedings he confessed to shooting at William Macro. He also acknowledged that the only reason he escaped no further than *The Bull* at Kentford was because his horse collapsed with fatigue on the road to the inn. His admission helped to seal his fate, the other evidence being described by the trial judge as a connected chain of events rather than positive proof of his guilt. Shocked by the attempt on the life of the well-respected farmer, Steggles was given the sentence of death for his crime.

On the morning of Wednesday, 2 April, James Steggles faced the hangman's noose in Bury St Edmunds. Samuel Oxer, the burglar and former private in the East Suffolk Militia who had earlier escaped his prison cell, was also executed, as was Samuel Roberts, one of the highwaymen brought up from London.

It would be many years before the threat and fear of highway robbery would disappear from the roads and lanes of the Suffolk countryside. In the remaining years of the eighteenth century no fewer than seven men would face execution for the same crime – testament perhaps to William Fennor's earlier observations about the prevalence of these desperate and ruthless criminals.

CHAPTER 3

A Family Affair
(1793)

As she began to yell, he continued to bring the wooden stake down onto Sarah's head, her attempts to deflect the blows with her arms gradually subsiding until she had been rendered unconscious . . .

When Sarah Nichols entered the taproom of the *Fox Inn* in Honington sometime before eight o'clock on the evening of Saturday, 14 September 1793, the landlord, William Pendle, barely raised an eyebrow. The 16-year-old girl from the nearby village of Fakenham Magna had set off from her home as the sun was beginning to set in order to buy 'a poke' of flour from the rural alehouse. She

The Fox Inn, *Honington, where Sarah Nichols purchased a bag of flour before being beaten to death with a hedge stake on 14 September 1793.*

was a regular customer, and having purchased the three-stone bag of flour and some thread for darning, set off in the dark to walk the lonely mile back to her family home. It was the last time that anyone outside of her family would see the young woman alive.

Early the next morning a passer-by spotted a bonnet, cap and shoe lying on the road to Honington, close to the gate that marked the parish boundary. Exciting some interest, there was early speculation that these might belong to Sarah Nichols, as they were recognized by her younger sister, Elizabeth, who confirmed that the girl had failed to return home the night before. Elizabeth was making her way into Honington to find out what had become of Sarah.

At ten o'clock the same morning, the fate of the young girl became clear when Sarah's dead body was found lying in a deep ditch beside the road. It was discovered by William Pendle as he was riding out in the direction of Thetford. While her head could be seen, it was clear that she had been dead for some time,

The lonely road into Fakenham Magna, where Sarah Nichols was murdered.

her open mouth being full of congealed blood and already plagued by flies. Her clothes were pulled up over her body. The horrified landlord rode back into Honington to alert the village and asked a couple of local women to attend to the body. He then proceeded in the direction of Fakenham to break the terrible news to the Nichols family.

Arriving at the house, in the south end of the village, Pendle found Sarah's father, John Nichols, and her 19-year-old brother Nathaniel, working outside of the cottage. Their reaction to the news was not what Pendle had expected. John merely exclaimed, 'Dead! Lord have mercy on me!' He then called to Nathan and the pair headed off on foot to reclaim the body. It was the first indication that the two knew more than they were disclosing – Pendle had not even communicated at that point where the body had been found.

The family's apparent indifference to the death was noted by others in the village. John Bolingbroke helped John and Nathan to lay Sarah's body on a wooden plank, when he saw them removing the corpse from the ditch. Having assisted the two in carrying the body back to their cottage, he remained there for about half an hour, during which time the family displayed no emotion and expressed no concern about the unfortunate girl's demise. Later, when John was in the process of constructing a makeshift coffin for his daughter, he was overheard to say, 'Here's a cursed piece of work before a hanging.'

In contrast, there was an overwhelming sense of horror and outrage in the village when it became clear that Sarah had been murdered. The wagging tongues also began to suggest that John and Nathan were guilty of the crime.

The coroner's inquest into the death began on Tuesday, 17 September and ran for a period of two weeks. A post-mortem was carried out on that first day by John Mell, a doctor from Bardwell, some three miles south-east of Fakenham. When collected from the Nichols's cottage, the corpse was found in an upstairs room, unwashed and still laid out on the wooden plank. In his examination, Mell found that one of Sarah's garters had been removed from her leg and tied tightly around her throat, suggesting strangulation. There was no sign of any sexual assault, and the state of her skull, face and arms led him to conclude that Sarah had been beaten to death, while trying to defend herself. She was finally laid to rest in the churchyard of St Peter's the following day.

At the conclusion of the coroner's inquest, John and Nathan Nichols were arrested on suspicion of wilful murder and taken to Ipswich Gaol to await trial at the Lent Assizes. They were held in separate cells as the investigations against them continued.

John Nichols was found to be a stern, disagreeable man, who appeared largely indifferent to the charges brought against him. Born in the early 1730s, the hedge carpenter was a talented tradesman who had arrived in Fakenham with his family some thirty years earlier. Like most of the villagers, he worked for the Duke of Grafton, who owned the bulk of the land in and around the parish. John had been married three times, his wives producing between them at least eleven children, eight of whom had survived beyond infancy. The two oldest offspring, John and Mary, had both left home to start families of their own. John's third wife, Mary Snelling, was stepmother to both Nathan and Sarah – their own mother having died in 1778.

Following in his father's footsteps, Nathan Nichols had also become an outdoor carpenter employed on the Grafton estate. Alongside his domineering parent, he appeared to be gullible and easily influenced. And like his siblings, Nathan had not been blessed with the greatest of intellects. Isolated in his prison cell for over a month, with plenty of time to think about what he had done, it perhaps comes as no surprise that it was Nathan who first alerted the authorities to the manner in which his sister had died.

On Friday, 25 October 1793, Nathan asked to see John Ripshaw, the gaoler, and during his subsequent confession gave a full account of what had occurred that fateful night in September. According to the carpenter, he had been outside when Sarah left the cottage and headed off towards the *Fox Inn*. His father came out of their home shortly afterwards and met Nathan on the road to Honington. The pair then followed in the same direction as Sarah, walking towards the neighbouring village. At one point, John removed a wooden stake from the hedge beside the road.

By the time John and Nathan reached Taylor's Grove, a small area of woodland at the edge of the parish boundary, they could see Sarah up ahead, returning with the bag of flour. John then passed the hedge stake to Nathan and instructed him to attack his sister. Faced with the swearing and intimidation of his father, Nathan moved towards Sarah and sent her to the ground with the first blow from the stake. As she began to yell, he continued to bring the wooden stake down onto Sarah's head, her attempts to deflect the blows with her arms gradually subsiding until she had been rendered unconscious. The two men then ran back to Fakenham, his father scattering the flour into a field and warning Nathan to keep quiet about what they had done.

A number of witnesses would later testify that they had seen John and Nathan on the road to Honington at the time suggested. Two of the Nichols children would also claim that the pair had arrived home for supper at around eight o'clock that evening, with Nathan acting strangely and spilling his food on more than one occasion. At one point, the two men talked in whispers and Nathan left the cottage once more, returning much later that night.

By his own confession, Nathan returned to where they had left Sarah, intent on hiding her body. He claimed that she was still alive at this point. His father had suggested that he remove one of her garters and tie this around her neck to give the impression that she had strangled herself. This he did, before dragging his sister's body into a ditch and leaving her for dead.

William Day, a local man who knew Nathan, passed him as he headed back home a second time. His later testimony would prove crucial in placing the carpenter at the crime scene on the night of the murder. Nathan concluded his confession by saying that his father had agreed to give him a new pocket watch for continuing to keep silent about the affair.

Having heard the statement, John Ripshaw left Nathan in his cell and confronted John Nichols with the confession. The older man flatly denied any involvement in the crime. Ripshaw then marched Nathan to his father's cell and made him repeat the confession. Still John would not yield.

The trial of the two men began in Bury St Edmunds on Monday, 24 March 1794. The judge was Sir William Ashurst. William Pendle and John Bolinbroke were the first witnesses called. Both outlined how the body had been discovered. Surgeon John Mell went on to describe the results of his post-mortem and his conclusions about the manner of death. Other witnesses were called to testify about the discovery of items of Sarah's clothing on the morning after the murder.

While largely circumstantial, the evidence given by the numerous witnesses was comprehensive. John Nichols's daughters, Elizabeth and Susanna, described how they had been in the family cottage on the night in question and had seen both men return home for supper, with Nathan acting oddly. Four independent witnesses recalled seeing Nathan in Fakenham that night which, when combined with his own confession, meant that the case against the younger man was particularly strong. The court also heard that Nathan had repeated his confession a second time to Francis Newberry, a fellow worker on the Grafton estate, who had visited him in the gaol.

It also emerged during the trial that Sarah had been frequently ill-treated by her family. Her father had been heard to strike the young woman in spite of her pleas not to be hit. Nathan had also been seen swearing at his sister and hitting her on one occasion, while another witness testified that she had seen bruising on the girl's arm prior to the murder.

Having no counsel to represent them, John and Nathan were both called to give evidence and conduct their own defence. For his part, John Nichols did little to refute the charges against him, claiming only that he was innocent of the crime and choosing not to question any of the witnesses produced by the court. Nathan repeated his earlier confession.

In his summing up, Sir William Ashurst made it clear that the confession alone was not sufficient to condemn the men. However, when taken alongside all the circumstantial evidence and the clear indifference shown by the family to Sarah's death, he indicated that there were good grounds for believing that the men were guilty as charged. Furthermore, he contended that all the evidence pointed to this being a crime of hatred.

The jury took only a short time to reach its verdict of 'guilty'. Sir William then sentenced both father and son to death, further directing that after the execution John should be hanged in chains, close to the murder scene, and Nathan should be dissected for future medical research. Four other prisoners, who were tried and capitally convicted on the same day, also received the death penalty.

Gossip in the village, though not emerging during the trial, was that there may have been a sexual motive for the murder. Stories began to circulate that Sarah had been pregnant when she was killed and the rumours were that either John or Nathan had been responsible. Perhaps she had been murdered to prevent the scandal of her pregnancy from being known about in the village.

The execution of the Nichols men was planned to take place within forty-eight hours of their conviction, on Wednesday, 26 March. However, on the Tuesday evening, while still in his condemned cell, Nathan announced to his gaolers that the confession he had given had been false. The local magistrate, Capel Lofft, was called and proceeded to question Nathan with two lawyers and two men from the gaol.

At first, the carpenter asserted that his father was innocent and claimed that he had only confessed because he thought that this would prevent both men from being executed. However, when challenged on his new testimony, he went on to admit that he had been told by his father to withdraw the confession at this late stage. Eventually, he confirmed that the original confession had been accurate, but added that his stepmother had played a part in the crime. He alleged that in the week before the murder she had provoked John into action by saying that he 'must do something with the girl, for she could do nothing with her'. Accurate or not, no steps were taken to bring charges against the stepmother.

Both men were eventually hanged from a tree on Thingoe Hill, north of Bury St Edmunds, at ten o'clock on Wednesday, 2 April. Many thousands of spectators had gathered to witness the execution. Nathan was still admitting his guilt, while John steadfastly refused to acknowledge that he had played any part in the murder. When he stood upon the gallows he appeared relaxed and unmoved, shaking hands with his son and throwing his hat and neckerchief into the crowd. When the appointed time came, he gave a short speech saying that while he was innocent, he bore no malice towards his son.

After the execution, and in line with the judge's direction, Nathan's body was carried to the Shire Hall in Bury St Edmunds to be anatomized. His father's corpse was taken by cart to Fakenham, where it was hung in an iron cage, as part of a purpose-built gibbet, at the scene of the murder. Over the coming weeks it was visited by many thousands of onlookers.

The story of John Nichols's body did not end there however. When his flesh had rotted away, the dead man was buried in a pit in the grounds of Willow Hall, at the outer reaches of the parish of Honington. This became the site of the Honington airbase, which officially opened in May 1937, to play an important role in the Allied bombing campaign against Nazi Germany during the Second World War. Later, it became home to the famous 'V-bombers' (Valient and Victor aircraft) of the Cold War.

During 1938, when the runway of the airbase was being extended, the gibbet cage was dug up to the astonishment of the construction workers involved. Inside was the skeleton of the executed man, the soles of his leather shoes still intact. While his body was eventually reburied, the iron gibbet cage was given to Moyse's Hall Museum in Bury St Edmunds, where it is displayed to this day as a lasting and telling reminder of eighteenth-century criminal justice.

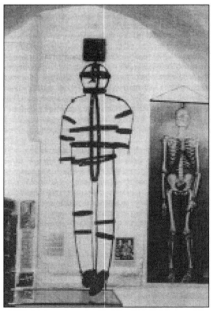

The iron gibbet cage used to hang the body of John Nichols, as preserved in Moyse's Hall Museum, Bury St Edmunds. Suffolk Local History Council

CHAPTER 4

The Baronet and the Body-Snatchers
(1826)

The two body-snatchers had brought with them all of the tools of their macabre trade – a sack and box for the body, wooden spades . . . and a selection of chisels, crowbars, bradawls and files . . .

Grave-robbing for medical research purposes has a surprisingly long history, extending back to at least 1540 when Henry VIII granted a royal charter to the Company of Barber-Surgeons, allowing them the right to claim the bodies of four executed criminals each year for dissection at lectures or demonstrations. From that time, the need to understand and dissect the workings of the human body continued to grow, as did the shortage of subjects for the research. It was only a matter of time before more inventive solutions would be found to this problem of supply and demand, and in the late eighteenth and early nineteenth century the gap was filled by body-snatchers. For their part, the eastern counties were to become a familiar hunting ground for these unscrupulous purveyors of human flesh.

One of the most prolific offenders was Thomas Vaughan, an East Anglian body-snatcher who was arrested in Beccles along with two other men and brought to trial in Norwich for a string of grave-robbing offences. His punishment was six months in prison – a sentence that reflects the inadequacies of the criminal justice system in being able to deal with these offenders. Technically, it was not illegal to disinter a body. As a corpse was deemed to belong to no one, logically it could not be stolen. The body-snatchers were careful not to steal shrouds, grave goods or coffins, so their punishment was often only a fine or, at worst, six months in prison. With fresh corpses fetching as much as £10 each, their's was a rewarding day's work, with comparatively few risks.

The panic caused by the growing number of body thefts led many Suffolk people to take action to prevent the graves of their loved ones being desecrated. High iron railings and gates that could be locked at night were erected in some graveyards. A good example of an anti-body-snatching device can be found in the churchyard of St Botolph in Burgh. This contains a low tomb chest enclosed in a spiked cage – the latter dug six feet into the ground.

For the same reason, graves were often dug deeper than normal and night watchmen, sometimes accommodated in purpose-built watch houses, were occasionally employed by wealthier citizens to outwit the body-snatchers. The thieves responded by raiding the graveyards of isolated communities and areas that could not afford the more expensive measures required to fend them off. Poor graves tended to be the most sought after, as paupers were often buried in mass graves that were left uncovered until they were full of coffins.

Anti-body-snatching device in the churchyard of St Botolph, Burgh.

The apparent ease with which the grave-robbers managed to ply their trade added greatly to the fear of local communities. On the night of Tuesday, 13 November 1821, body-snatchers entered the churchyard of St Mary's in Woodbridge and dug up and stole the body of the recently deceased wife of local man Captain Forman. Despite the offer of a £15 reward, no one was ever caught for this act of desecration.

This case caused a wave of hysteria in many villages close to Woodbridge, best illustrated by a story linked to a gravestone in

Gravestone of Robert Manby and Mary King in the churchyard of St Edmund, Bromeswell.

the churchyard of St Edmund in Bromeswell. The gravestone marks the burial of Robert Manby and Mary King. Mary died of consumption in December 1822 and just before her death, fearful of the body-snatchers, she pleaded with Robert to watch over her grave. He did so every night after her burial until the grief of his loss became too strong. He took his own life in June 1823 by rowing out into the Deben estuary one night and drowning himself.

The demand for fresh corpses came from teaching hospitals and medical schools, and it was the gallows that supplied the only legal supply of cadavers in the early eighteenth century. With the medical profession requiring around 500 bodies each year and executions delivering typically less than sixty, it is easy to see how unprincipled surgeons were willing to obtain corpses from almost any source, including those supplied by the so-called resurrectionists.

Alongside Cambridge University, all the major London hospitals had their own programmes of teaching and anatomical research. These institutions became heavily reliant on the acquisition of cadavers from body-snatchers. One of the best-connected surgeons in this respect was Sir Astley Paston Cooper, who, operating at Guy's Hospital, achieved wealth, status and kudos in the medical community for his unrivalled skills with the scalpel. Operating with speed and accuracy, and without antiseptics or anaesthesia, Cooper became a favourite of both the rich and the poor for his medical abilities. But, as he would later admit, he owed much of his success to his life-long relationship with a small, but proficient, band of grave-robbers.

Born in 1768, Astley Cooper was the son of a Norfolk clergyman, and his career knew no limits. He was a surgeon to three successive monarchs, a doctor to the Duke of Wellington and served twice as president of the Royal College of Surgeons. In 1821, he was honoured with a baronetcy for removing a cyst from the scalp of King George IV. By that stage he was reputed to be

Sir Astley Paston Cooper

earning £21,000 a year – around £1.5 million in today's money – making him easily the highest-paid surgeon of his time.

Cooper spent a considerable amount of time on the dissecting table, gaining an unparalleled knowledge of anatomy and physiology. But his craft demanded a constant supply of bodies on which to learn and experiment. For this he relied on a network of exhumers, who were willing and able to deliver the corpses of men, women and children to the back door of his dissecting room. To ensure that he got the best supply in this competitive black market, Cooper invested in night workers, advancing them money to cover the initial investment in picks and shovels and always paying the best price for a fresh corpse. He stuck to his band of body-snatchers, even through their periods of sickness or drunkenness, and paid for their legal representation when required. He was also known to have supported the families of some grave-robbers who faced prison sentences for their crimes.

That Cooper was able to direct and control his loyal gang of grave-robbers is best illustrated by his testimony to a Commons Select Committee in 1828, which was set up to investigate the growing problem of body-snatching. Reflecting on his associations with the exhumers, Cooper said: 'The law does not prevent us from obtaining the body of an individual if we think proper; for there is no person, let his situation in life be what it may, whom, if I was disposed to dissect, I could not obtain. Nobody is secured by the law; it only adds to the price . . . '

While his comments smack of arrogance, they were probably honest and accurate in describing the general inability of the law to counter the threat of body-snatching at that time. In fact, Cooper had successfully demonstrated his ability to obtain a specific body he was 'disposed to dissect' two years before – a bizarre and fascinating case involving the body of a Suffolk man.

William Cowles was a 39-year-old gardener from Beccles who was suffering from a painful swelling in the main artery of his groin. He was unable to find a surgeon locally who could treat his condition and in any case had no money to pay for such an operation. Hopeful that Astley Cooper could operate on him, Cowles took a coach to London in June 1808. Sleeping fitfully on the roof of the coach did little for his condition and on arrival in the capital Cowles found that the swelling in his groin had grown. When he was examined by Cooper the next day at Guy's Hospital, the skin was beginning to discolour and turn gangrenous. After a gruelling operation the same day, the eminent surgeon saved Cowles's life.

Cooper was so keen to revisit this pioneering piece of surgery that he arranged for Cowles's whereabouts to be tracked over the course of the man's life. Even though the gardener travelled around a fair deal, each local doctor would always correspond with the medical practitioner of the next place he moved to. Unbeknown to Cowles, his passage through life was well documented, although those years would turn out to be spectacularly uneventful.

Cowles's wanderings led him eventually to the Heckingham workhouse, some seven miles from his hometown of Beccles. This had been built in 1765 with facilities for the reception of 'aged, sick or infirm persons and young children, as are not able to work', together with a 'house of correction for punishing and keeping to hard labour such idle or disorderly persons who being able shall refuse to work or otherwise misbehave themselves'. How Cowles fared under this regime we can only surmise, but he died there in June 1826 'friendless and worn out'. He was buried in the workhouse cemetery.

Henchman Crowfoot, a doctor in Beccles, wrote to Astley Cooper when he learned of Cowles's demise. On hearing the news, Cooper dispatched two of his most trusted body-snatchers to travel to Suffolk the next evening in order to obtain the gardener's body.

John Bishop, a literate 28-year-old former carrier from Highgate in London, had been a body-snatcher for around seven years. Married with two young sons at that time, he had been responsible for obtaining and selling over 500 bodies to the main London teaching hospitals. His accomplice was his son-in-law, Thomas Williams, a 21-year-old bricklayer by trade who, like Bishop, enjoyed a drink and smoked a pipe. The pair had already worked for Astley Cooper many times.

Arriving at Henchman Crowfoot's house in Beccles, the two body-snatchers had brought with them all of the tools of their macabre trade – a sack and box for the body, wooden spades which were less noisy for digging and a selection of chisels, crowbars, bradawls and files for opening whatever coffin they might encounter. Setting off for the cemetery at around eleven o'clock by horse-drawn cart, the two were joined by Crowfoot and his assistant and another man who lodged with the surgeon.

The body-snatchers would have worked in darkness and at speed on that quiet, warm, summer's evening. Removing the newly laid, uncompacted soil from the head end of the grave, the two men would have left the rest of the plot covered while they removed the body. This skilled task involved prising open the lid of the coffin and lifting it against the weight of the soil to enable the body to be pulled out head first. As Cowles was buried as a pauper, it was quite possible that his body would have been buried without a coffin, making the job even easier. The men then placed the body in a sack and tidied up to leave no trace of the exhumation. The corpse was taken back to Crowfoot's house to be transferred into the box brought by the exhumers. From here the two men said their goodbyes and headed off back to London. Their night's work went undetected.

Cooper was delighted to receive the cadaver and wasted no time in getting it onto the dissecting table. It was almost eighteen years to the day that he had first operated on William Cowles and he was thrilled to see that his earlier surgery had resulted in the growth of new blood vessels which had kept the Suffolk gardener healthy for the remaining years of his life. So pleased was he with his work that he had Cowles's dissected leg mounted for display: it can still be seen at Guy's Hospital.

Over time, the insatiable demands of surgeons like Cooper were addressed through a more legitimate supply of corpses. Parliament enacted legislation to allow people to specify in their wills that their bodies could be used for medical research. The Anatomy Act of 1832 also allowed for the bodies of unknown and unclaimed individuals to be used for dissection. In effect, this meant that if no one claimed you, or if your family could not afford to bury you properly, the authorities could send your body to the surgeons. Although this legislation reduced the practice of illegal grave-robbing, it did little to remove the disgust and fear that many poor people had of being claimed by the body-snatchers after their death.

This continuing fear is best illustrated by a case reported by the *Bury and Norwich Post* on 1 July 1846. The report outlines how the body of Mary Plumb, a young woman who had died in the Union House in Sudbury a week before, had been taken to a nearby parish for burial. Believing that her body had been retained at the Union House for the purposes of medical dissection, and that the coffin therefore contained nothing but stones and rubbish, a number of local people intercepted the hearse and insisted on opening the coffin. Their action succeeded only in confirming that the casket did contain the putrefying remains of the unfortunate young woman who had died as a result of disease.

Astley Cooper died on the afternoon of 12 February 1841. Having built a career by dissecting countless dead bodies, he left clear instructions for his own corpse to be medically examined after his death. His surgeon colleagues complied with his wishes, and as well as probing all the matters suggested by the man himself, concluded that the most likely cause of his death had been heart failure. Unlike the unfortunate subjects on which Cooper and others preyed with such apparent freedom, however, his body was entombed within a stone sarcophagus, deep within a crypt below the chapel at Guy's Hospital. He had little to fear from the body-snatchers.

In contrast, the grave-robbers John Bishop and Thomas Williams met their death some ten years before Cooper in circumstances that could not have been more distinct. In the autumn of 1831, both men were arrested with a fellow body-snatcher called James May for attempting to sell the body of a 14-year-old boy to surgeon Richard Partridge at King's College London. Having examined the body, Partridge had his suspicions and called for the police. A post-mortem showed that the spine had been damaged and there was no evidence that the body had been interred, suggesting that the men had in fact murdered the boy.

When quizzed about how they came to be in possession of the body, Bishop is alleged to have cried, 'I am a bloody body-snatcher!' His home at 3 Nova Scotia Gardens, in the East End of London, was found to contain all the tools of his trade, and the men did not deny that they were professional resurrectionists. The yard of the home which the Bishops shared with Williams and his family had been used to store the bodies they had obtained. At their trial at the Old Bailey on Thursday, 1

December 1831, all three men were convicted and sentenced to death for killing what was believed to be an immigrant from Piedmont by the name of Carlo Ferrari, alias Charles Ferrier. The crime came to be known as 'The Italian Boy Murder'.

The body-snatchers' method of killing this and other victims was to administer either alcohol or opium and then to drop them head first into a garden well to drown. After their conviction, Bishop confessed to the killing and stated, 'I have

Extract from the confession letter written by body-snatcher John Bishop.
The National Archives

followed the course of obtaining a livelihood as a body-snatcher for twelve years and have obtained and sold I think from 500 to 1,000 bodies.' He then goes on to describe the nature of the crime:

> *Whilst Williams held the cord to prevent his body going altogether too low into the well – he was nearly wholly in the water of the well – his feet just above the surface. Williams fastened the other end of the cord round the paling to prevent the body getting out of reach. The boy struggled a bit with his arms and legs in the water – and the water bubbled for a minute – we waited.*

There were two ironies in the undoing of the body-snatchers in this case. The first was that given their track record in obtaining hundreds of bodies by dubious means, it was by no means certain that the corpse was indeed that of the missing

Italian; the evidence of his identity was indeed shaky. The gang later claimed that the body was that of a young man from Lincolnshire who had been driving cattle to Smithfield.

The second irony was to be the manner of their deaths. While May's sentence was commuted to transportation for life, he was sent to a prison hulk in preparation for the voyage to Australia. He never made the journey, but died in the hold of the ship before leaving England. Bishop and Williams were hanged at Newgate on Monday, 5 December before a crowd of 30,000. Bishop died quickly, his neck having been broken by the drop. Williams suffered more, the noose eventually strangling him when his strength gave out. Fittingly, both men were then taken away for dissection. As the fitter and better proportioned of the two, Bishop's body was taken to King's College for public display and anatomization. He was described as being a fine specimen – the sort of physique that could earn a body-snatcher good money in fact.

Chapter 5

A Double Murder in Milden
(1828)
'My ruin was being acquainted with them girls next door.'

There can be few crimes more horrific than the murder of a child. Alongside the more common crime of infanticide, there were at least twenty child killings in England that resulted in a public execution during the nineteenth century. One of these was the largely overlooked double murder of two young brothers in the pretty village of Milden, some five miles north of Sudbury in the hundred of Babergh. What made this case particularly shocking was the gap between the two murders, the second occurring well over a year after the first. And while the story contains a potent blend of misguided love, blackmail and unfathomable cruelty, its main ingredient appears to have been chance – the quirky, and in this case deadly, consequences of being in the wrong place at the wrong time.

By all accounts, George Partridge was not the brightest pupil in the class. Born in Milden in 1807, one of eighteen children, the 23-year-old may not have had the best of starts in life. His parents, William and Elizabeth Partridge, were considered to be of 'good character' but struggled, in an endless cycle of rural poverty, to put food in the mouths of their numerous offspring. Unable to read or write, prone to aggression and easily influenced by others, George soon fell in with the wrong crowd and began to indulge in petty crime to support himself and his family.

The trouble began when the young farm labourer became sweet on Elizabeth or 'Bet' Phillips, one of three teenage girls who lived next door to the Partridges. The girls appeared to be very aware of their sexual allure, even attending a local Methodist group purely to meet the young men of the village. Many of the crimes that Partridge committed were inspired by the girls, and the family as a whole appeared to be more than willing to turn a blind eye to the law.

It was on Wednesday, 1 August 1827, that the convoluted series of events began to unfold. Jonas Ansell, the 6-year-old son of a local farmer, was unfortunate enough to catch the hapless George Partridge in a compromising position with his promiscuous girlfriend. Since Jonas had seen more than Bet wished him to, it was later claimed that she urged Partridge to kill the boy. At first he refused to act, but when Bet apparently promised to yield to his desires as often as he liked and with no strings attached, Partridge took the knife offered by his young lover and set out to kill the farmer's son.

Partridge found Jonas Ansell sitting on the brow of a ditch near an osier bed (a small plantation of willows used for basket-making). The lad's jacket lay on the ground beside him. By his own admission, Partridge then attacked the boy, stabbing him to death. Jonas struggled and made some noise, but was soon silenced by his attacker. Partridge then returned the knife to Bet Phillips.

Road leading into the village of Milden, the scene of a double murder in the 1820s.

While the fatal assault was taking place, Partridge was being watched by two small boys, younger brothers of Bet Phillips. He had seen them in the distance but assumed they had not seen him. Finding the dead body of young Ansell a little later, John and Robert Phillips ran home to tell their sister what Partridge had done, unaware perhaps that she had been, in all likelihood, the architect of the murder plan.

Fearful of the consequences of being implicated in the crime, Bet Phillips made her way to the murder scene to hide the body. She was helped by her own mother. Between them they put the jacket back on Jonas and carried his lifeless body into an oat field. Later that evening they returned once more, transferring the body into the osier bed where it was discovered a few days later.

In the aftermath of the stabbing, suspicion fell on George Partridge, but he was not charged. Bet's mother and two brothers were jailed, however, and charged with being accessories to the murder. At the inquest held at nearby Monks

The village of Monks Eleigh, where the coroner's inquest into the death of Jonas Ansell was held in August 1827.

Eleigh later that month, the jury heard from a local surgeon that Jonas Ansell had died from a three-inch stab wound to his back. It was suggested that someone had put the boy's jacket back on him after death, as blood had been found near where the body first lay, but not on his clothes. There was also found to be severe bruising on the boy's forehead.

The Phillips family gave contradictory statements about their own whereabouts on the day of the murder. Mrs Phillips's three teenage daughters swore positively that their mother had not left home the whole day. However, one of the brothers claimed he had been bathing with Jonas Ansell earlier in the day, had struck him with a stick and had watched him sink in the water. He further claimed that his mother had retrieved the boy's body from the water.

In the event, the inquest jury returned a verdict of wilful murder by persons unknown. It seemed as if George Partridge had escaped any form of justice for his callous act. Jonas Ansell was buried in the village churchyard on Wednesday, 8 August.

But events then took an unlikely turn as Partridge found himself subject to a blackmailing campaign by the unscrupulous Phillips family. For over a year, they extorted money from him, periodically threatening to inform against him if he did not pay up. Desperate for money and occasionally unable even to pay his father for board and lodgings, Partridge took to increasing levels of thieving in order to silence his tormentors.

Set against the backdrop of events elsewhere in Suffolk at that time, it is easy to see why Partridge continued to take the blackmail threats seriously. In April 1828, the police formally arrested William Corder for the murder of Maria Marten in the *Red Barn* at Polstead. The widely publicized murder trial that followed was big news nationally and must have been the subject of much gossip in Milden, a village only seven miles from the scene of Corder's infamous deed. The greatest irony of all was the fact that Partridge actually watched the hanging of Corder in the grounds of Bury St Edmunds Prison on 11 August 1828, only eight months before he would stand on the same gallows himself, convicted of the murder of Robert Ansell's son. The only surprise was that it was not Jonas Ansell for whom Partridge was to swing.

Partridge's thieving led to his eventual undoing, but it was a particularly cruel twist of fate that the only witness to his crime should be George Ansell, the 9-year-old brother of young Jonas. On Tuesday, 4 November 1828, Partridge was seen by Ansell stealing lambs from a nearby farm owned by a Mr Woodgate. Catching the boy, Partridge cut his throat from ear to ear with as little regard as he had demonstrated in the earlier killing of the younger brother, Jonas.

George Ansell's body was found by his father a few hours later. Police Constable Thomas Bowers was called to the scene and a search of the area was conducted. George Partridge was detained by PC Bowers near Langley Wood, Preston St Mary, carrying a blood-stained knife. His slop frock also had visible bloodstains on it. He was immediately arrested on suspicion of murder, and on the orders of the local magistrate was held until the coroner arrived.

In the investigation that followed, Partridge very nearly escaped justice a second time. PC Bowers had retained the murder weapon in his pocket and when it was presented for examination a couple of days later, the blood stains on the blade had all but been erased. In fact, there was little evidence to link Partridge to the crime. Desperate to get a result, the police arranged for the prisoner to be taken to the crime scene, where Partridge's composure finally broke and he confessed to the killing. He claimed that the boy had been cheeky to him and he had lost his temper. He was committed to Bury St Edmunds Prison charged with the wilful murder of George Ansell.

Throughout his eventual trial at the Suffolk Assizes in the Shire Hall of Bury St Edmunds, George Partridge displayed no remorse or regrets for his actions. Having confessed to killing George Ansell there could be only one outcome and Partridge was duly convicted of murder and sentenced to be hanged. On being returned to his cell after the trial he was stripped of his clothes and dressed in the uniform of a condemned man. His own clothes were then distributed between his brothers.

In the days immediately following the trial, Partridge had plenty of time for reflection, although the Reverend West, acting as temporary chaplain to the prison, noted that he continued to show no emotion during religious services. Only when he was brought a message from his sister Susan by the Reverend Hallward, curate of Milden, did the prisoner appear to be outwardly affected.

On Saturday, 11 April 1829, Partridge was visited by another clergyman, the Reverend J Smyth. With the sentence of death passed and no hope of reprieve, Partridge finally confessed to killing Jonas Ansell in addition to the boy's older brother. The following day he was visited by his parents and five of his brothers and sisters. Confronted by his father, who had heard reports of Partridge's second confession, George admitted, 'Yes father, I killed both boys.' His father then enquired, 'Good God, George, how came you to do that? I would have laid my life you never did it,' to which his son replied, 'Oh father! My ruin was being acquainted with them girls next door,' before going on to explain how he had been criminally connected with all three teenagers and Bet Phillips in particular.

On Monday morning, the day of the execution, Partridge was visited by four more of his family before being taken to the Press Room of Bury Prison just before midday to reassert his earlier confession. He was then walked around the prison to shake hands with the other inmates, many of whom appeared to be overcome by Partridge's situation. He retained the same sullen and unyielding composure. The governor of the prison, Mr Orridge, later described him as 'rather dull, having a down-like and slow intellect'.

When he was later led to the scaffold, the assembled crowd of several thousand spectators was told that the condemned man had confessed to killing both the Ansell brothers. The rope was then secured and, once the burial service had been read, the ill-fated George Partridge was dispatched by the hangman in the customary way. Reports in the local press afterwards indicated that 'not a single struggle was observed, except a slight heaving of the chest after a lapse of several minutes'.

When the execution crowd had dispersed, the dead man's body was cut down after an hour and transported to the Shire Hall in Bury St Edmunds. Here it was put on public display: the corpse was laid out on a table with all the skin removed to reveal the muscles of the thorax. Later that evening, in accordance with the special warrant issued by the trial judge, the body was moved to Suffolk Hospital, where it was dissected for medical research.

Like other cases of child murder in the nineteenth century, the killing of George Ansell became the subject of a broadsheet ballad recounting the nature of the crime in some detail. Among the verses of this particular ballad were the telling lines:

The worthy rector sought the wretch
With prayer and peace to bless,
And to the worthy man he did
His guilty deeds confess.

Given that it occurred only months after the sensational coverage of the *Red Barn* murder, it is surprising that the killing of the Ansell brothers, with all the twists and turns that the story entailed, did not excite more interest in the local and national press. Then, as now, the tale remains a chilling, if little-known, example of murder most foul.

CHAPTER 6

The Drowning of Mrs Bainbridge
(1851)
'The halter is for my neck . . . the gallows is my doom.'

Unrequited love can be a powerful and destructive emotion. It was something that Elizabeth Bainbridge knew all about, having been left by her husband of only two years and forced to return to her family home in 1843 when the quarrelling and domestic abuse reached breaking point. However, it was the unrequited love of a future suitor that would ultimately seal her fate – a crime of passion that in 1851 would also see a 23-year-old farm labourer hanged for Elizabeth's murder. This was to be the last man to be executed in Bury St Edmunds.

Elizabeth Payne was born in 1821 and entered domestic service at only 13 years of age. It was while working in the village of Edwardstone, some fourteen miles from the family home at Bradfield St Clare, that the 21-year-old Elizabeth met and married Thomas Bainbridge, a butler to the Reverend John Halifax of Edwardstone House. While the couple had a baby, their marriage was short-lived, with Elizabeth's father eventually convincing her to return with the child to the new family home in Lawshall to escape being ill-treated by Thomas. Elizabeth saw her husband only once more after that time. He enlisted in the Army in the Corps of Sappers and Miners and was posted to India, where he was eventually promoted to corporal.

Elizabeth Bainbridge settled back into family life in Lawshall, looking after her father, James Payne, and one of her brothers and working hard as a dressmaker and shoe binder. Her working day started at four o'clock each morning and she was recognized by everyone in the village as a decent and industrious woman. Another brother, William Payne, was landlord of the *Harrow Inn* public house in Lawshall where Elizabeth stayed in the week leading up to her death. It was here that she became acquainted with another of the lodgers at the inn, 23-year-old George Cant, the son of Lazarus and Mary Cant, a respectable working family in the village.

George Cant was a good-looking farm labourer of medium build with long, light coloured, hair. On first impression most people considered him to be quiet and inoffensive, although it was clear that he had a darker side to his character, as later events would prove. Cant was clearly besotted by Elizabeth Bainbridge and the two were seen 'walking out' together. He would later claim that they were lovers and that both were deeply unhappy about the fact that Elizabeth remained married and the two of them could therefore not wed. In reality, while Elizabeth was fond of Cant she was unable to return his affections and remained impassive to his protestations of love.

In addition to any emotional turmoil the young labourer may have felt, George Cant also suffered from frequent epileptic fits and blackouts and was given to heavy bouts of drinking. While hard working, he would later be described by the chaplain of Bury St Edmunds Prison as 'deplorably ignorant' with his 'moral senses . . . blunted by a long course of drunkenness and vice'.

On Monday, 20 January 1851 both Elizabeth Bainbridge and George Cant had been drinking at the *Harrow Inn*. Jane Clark, a barmaid, who also lived at the inn, knew both of them – all three had gone to Bury Fair together in October 1850. Jane remembered Elizabeth leaving the taproom at about three-thirty that afternoon to return to her father's house. She later claimed that Cant had left some five minutes after Elizabeth by another door. Both were seen by John Moss, another villager, about half an hour later, talking amiably and crossing a meadow owned by a Mr Reeman that contained a small pond.

William Payne, the landlord, returned from his father's house at about five o'clock that afternoon and was asked by his wife what time Elizabeth had returned home. Having not seen her, he was immediately concerned about his sister's wellbeing and sent a man back to his father's house to check that she had arrived home safely. The man returned with the answer 'No'.

At seven o'clock that evening George Cant arrived back at the *Harrow Inn*, his clothes dirty and wet, his hat missing and his shoes soaked and mud-filled. He appeared to be greatly agitated and largely incoherent to those drinking in the bar, and was immediately given some brandy. George Farrow, a fellow lodger at the inn, asked him what the matter was. Cant responded curtly: 'Pray, don't say anything to me. The halter is for my neck . . . the gallows is my doom.' While drinking his brandy and water he would only add that he was afraid it would be the last glass he would drink. Farrow then removed Cant's shoes and placed them in a back room.

Noticing that he was acting oddly, the landlord asked Cant where his hat was, to which the labourer replied, 'In the pond'. Knowing that he suffered from fits, the landlord remonstrated that he could not be trusted to 'blunder about' on his own in this way. Farrow then took Cant upstairs to his room, putting him to bed and looking in on him a couple of times afterwards. Cant appeared to be extremely unhappy and claimed a number of times that he had been 'got hold of by the devil'. He also said that his watch was in the pond.

Now even more concerned about Elizabeth's safety, William Payne sent for the local constable. Police Constable John Keeble arrived without delay, to be greeted by the landlord on the doorstep of the *Harrow Inn*. Payne was holding George Cant's soaked shoes and some of his wet clothes. Having exchanged a few brief words, PC Keeble hurried upstairs to Cant's room. When asked if he knew of Elizabeth's whereabouts, the labourer refused to answer.

PC Keeble then began a search for Elizabeth, involving her father and George Farrow. Holding a lantern, they traced George Cant's muddy footprints, which ran from a meadow opposite the inn. Beyond this they continued into Reeman's meadow and up to the left side of the pond where, amidst the weeds and mud, they found the dead body of Elizabeth Bainbridge. Her head was buried in the weeds and she lay in a foot and a half of muddy water. Keeble could see scratches on her face and a bruise above her right eye. There was also blood coming from her nose. Tied around the neck of the deceased was a bonnet ribbon holding a small watch. It was later claimed that this was a love token given to her by George Cant. In return, he had taken her wedding ring – it was found later in his purse.

Elizabeth's body was taken to a nearby house where it was examined by George King, a surgeon from Hartest. He observed

The pond in Lawshall where Elizabeth Bainbridge was drowned on Monday, 20 January 1851.

that the skin above the right eye was swollen, as if from a blow. Opening her closed mouth he could see evidence of frothing around the nose and teeth. He also noted the scratches on her face, and that there were bruises under the elbow of each arm and sand and mud under her fingernails. King believed that she had been held down under the water by another person and drowned.

When PC Keeble returned to the *Harrow Inn* and announced that the body had been found, Cant continued to be silent in response to questions. As a result, he was taken into custody.

A search of the murder scene was conducted next morning at first light. It was clear from the thorn bushes surrounding the pond that some sort of struggle had taken place. A couple of bramble branches were broken as if someone had been dragged through the bushes. Elizabeth's dress supported this assumption, having been torn from the gathers. Close by the searchers found a bundle containing Elizabeth's bonnet, handkerchief and cape, as well as the lead block she used for shoe binding. Crucially, they also found a man's hat similar to that worn by George Cant lying on the muddy bank, and footprints that matched Cant's shoes.

The murder inquiry was led by the aptly named Superintendent Oliver Death from Clare. He was convinced that Cant's motive for murder was jealousy, caused by Elizabeth's rejection of his affection. The prisoner initially denied any knowledge of the attack or Elizabeth's whereabouts. However, the police felt there was ample evidence to charge him with wilful murder, and when he came before the local magistrates later that month he was duly remanded to appear at the Suffolk Assizes at Bury St Edmunds in March 1851.

At his trial, the case against Cant proved overwhelming. Mr Prendergast for the prosecution called numerous witnesses who helped to piece together the chain of events leading to the drowning. The jury heard testimony about the times when the couple had been seen leaving the inn and talking on Reeman's meadow. Edward Harman, a new witness, who had not been called to give evidence to the local magistrates, said that he had been in the vicinity of the meadow on the afternoon in question and claimed to have heard the screams of a woman coming from the direction of the pond. Sadly, he also admitted taking 'no particular notice of them'.

A number of witnesses recounted seeing Cant return to the inn that evening soaked and acting suspiciously. George Farrow relayed his conversation with Cant about 'the gallows'. One witness recalled that when Cant was first told that the deceased's body had been found, he replied, 'Now I'm done'. Elizabeth's father explained how he had joined the search party and had found his daughter's body in the pond. And finally, there was the damning evidence of the surgeon, George King.

From the testimony given by PC Keeble, it also emerged that Cant had been involved in an earlier incident with a woman he had pursued. The police officer recollected that a couple of years before the drowning, Cant had to be physically manhandled away from a woman in Bury St Edmunds who shrieked 'Murder!' and announced that she would 'not go with him again'. Although Cant had not been charged with the assault, the event had lingered in the memories of many local people.

George Cant's defence was centred on his vulnerability to epileptic fits. The jury was told that on the day in question, he and Elizabeth Bainbridge had been in each other's company for several hours and had exchanged love tokens. As lovers, they had then made a suicide pact, desperately unhappy that they were unable to marry. It was claimed that as they walked across Reeman's meadow, Elizabeth had snatched a knife from Cant's pocket and after declaring that she could no longer bear to live, had put the knife to her throat. It was then alleged that when Cant prevented her cutting her throat, Elizabeth flung herself in the pond in an attempt to drown herself.

Mr Power, who led the defence counsel, then claimed that Cant had followed Elizabeth into the pond in a state of frenzy and, in spite of the woman's struggles and screams, had held her down in the water, overcome by his epilepsy. He had then intended to kill himself, but had no further recollection of the events that day until he found himself back at the *Harrow Inn* speaking to George Farrow.

Mr Image, the surgeon who had conducted the post-mortem, challenged the defence claims about the nature of Elizabeth's drowning. He explained that the instinctive nervous energy of a person held under the water by someone falling on top of them would be to struggle to reach the surface. This testimony laid bare the final plank of the defence case.

In summing up, the judge was scornful of the claims made by the prisoner and his defence counsel. 'It was a dreadful thing,' he said, 'thus to insult their [the jury's] common sense by asking them to credit such a baseless theory.' The jury took only a few minutes of deliberation, without leaving the box, to decide on a verdict of 'guilty'. The Lord Chief Justice then placed the black cap on his head before sentencing the prisoner to be hanged on 21 April 1851.

In the days that followed the trial, Cant showed every sign of remorse for his actions and sorrow for Elizabeth's death. It was claimed that he made frequent and unreserved confessions to the prison governor, Mr Macintyre, and to the prison chaplain – the latter describing Cant as 'very barren ground to work on'. Despite the claims, no written statement was produced. An application was also made to the Secretary of State, Sir George Grey, for remission of capital punishment on the grounds that there was no premeditation in the case. This failed: Sir George stated that he did not feel it consistent with his duty to grant remission and indicated that the law must take its course.

In the lead-up to the execution, the condemned man was visited by his cousins, two aunts, father, stepmother, brother

Lawshall Church, where Elizabeth Bainbridge was buried in 1851.

and little sister. On one visit, Cant noticed that one of his cousins had been drinking and turned on him adding, 'you know I was never a great drinker. I could never be called a drunkard. Let me implore you as a dying man, baptized at the same font as you, to avoid drunkenness.' He went on to talk about other crimes that had resulted from excesses of alcohol.

Other visitors included William Payne, Cant's former landlord. History has not recorded the nature of their conversation. Most visibly upset was George's father, who wept painfully at their final farewell. Cant leapt up to reassure his father with a spirited, 'Cheer up, old boy,' to which his father replied, 'George, if you had taken my advice, it would not have come to this.' His son responded with, 'That's true, but you don't know the temptations I've had.' He then asked where in Lawshall they had buried Elizabeth and, on being told, ventured, 'Poor thing, I am sorry for her. I knew it was wrong to live on the terms we did.'

Reports in the local press continued to claim that Cant had confessed to the crime, but no written document was ever produced to support this. One curious account in the *Suffolk Chronicle* described Cant as having a 'quite inoffensive disposition, quite incapable of perpetrating a deed of violence'.

The arrangements for the hanging at Bury St Edmunds Prison broke with tradition. Until that time, executions had always taken place in the meadow, on the south side of the prison, requiring the condemned to be taken out through the front entrance of the building and along a public road to the scaffold. The suitability of this had been reviewed following the earlier hanging of Catherine Foster, an 18-year-old woman who was executed on 17 April 1847 for poisoning her husband. The system was felt to be inappropriate, given the nearness of the spectators to the point of execution.

As a result of the revised arrangements, new gallows were constructed and placed on the roof between the infirmary on the south side of the prison and the entrance to the porter's lodge. The time of execution was also set earlier than normal, at nine o'clock in the morning, in an attempt to reduce the number of spectators likely to descend on the concourse. In the event, people began to arrive from six o'clock, as news of the earlier start had already circulated among the local population.

The execution took place one day later than planned, on Tuesday, 22 April 1851. The hangman that day was the celebrated William Calcraft, who became Britain's longest-serving executioner and is thought to have performed as many as 500 executions between 1829 and 1874. In addition to his fees for dispatching prisoners (typically £10 to £15), Calcraft was permitted to keep the clothes and personal effects of the condemned. These he often sold to Madame Tussaud's for dressing the waxworks in the Chamber of Horrors. There was also a reasonable resale value for the rope used to hang more notable criminals (up to 5 shillings or 25 pence an inch).

As the appointed time of the execution approached, all roads leading to the prison and every intervening field were occupied by eager spectators. Estimates at the time put the total attendance at around 5,000 people. The majority of these were women, often accompanied by children and infants, their enthusiasm barely dampened by the continuous rain, which fell until the point of execution.

Shortly after nine o'clock the death bell was sounded and George Cant was led from the condemned cell by a procession consisting of the sheriff, under sheriff, chaplain, governor and prison officers. As the chaplain delivered the appropriate lines from the burial service, Cant was dragged the final steps to the scaffold, moaning pitifully and looking very pale. Calcraft stepped forward to pinion the prisoner's arms and position him over the trap, at which point Cant's body appeared to be violently agitated. The rope was then adjusted to a staple fixed in the beam of the scaffold and a cap was drawn down over his face. At the appointed signal the chaplain closed his book, a bolt was drawn and with no visible struggle, George Cant fell through the trap to his death. A lone voice in the assembled crowd shouted, 'Hats off, umbrellas down!'

George Cant was buried in the precincts of the prison. To this day, the scene of the crime is often referred to as the 'Bainbridge Pond'.

CHAPTER 7

A Fashionable Crime

(1851)

Rollinson became increasingly detached and sullen and began to formulate more deadly plans to preserve what he thought was his by right . . .

For centuries, arsenic was the poison of choice for many killers who intended to dispatch their victims with a minimum of effort and in the hope that their actions would remain undetected. With little smell or taste, the poisonous white powder – which was obtained by heating arsenic sulphide – held a certain appeal for the cautious Victorian criminal. Used extensively for vermin control, it was widely available, the law requiring only that the purchaser sign the 'poison book' kept by every chemist and hardware supplier that stocked the toxic powder. And as the poison left no visible marks or blood and required no direct contact with the intended victim, arsenic poisoning became a frequent and insidious misdemeanour that challenged the criminal justice system and the evolving science of forensic pathology.

Suffolk saw its fair share of poisoning cases throughout the nineteenth century, and while few caught the public imagination as wholeheartedly as the case of Madeleine Smith – an aristocratic young woman from Glasgow who was accused of poisoning her lover with arsenic – they were, nevertheless, symptomatic of what many felt was a growing problem. This is best illustrated by the case of the west Suffolk poisoner, William Rollinson.

Rollinson (variously recorded as 'Rowlinson', 'Rawlinson' and even 'Robinson') was an 80-year-old farm labourer who lived in Sowley Green, about one and a half miles from Great Thurlow, not far from Haverhill. As a respected member of the community, Rollinson lived peacefully and frugally, and as a result of his infirmities and 'distressed position in life' was partly supported by the maintenance money he received from the parish. To supplement his income, he took to the roads – he was sometimes absent for a full day – to collect horse manure, which he would sell locally.

Rollinson's home was a detached, double tenement cottage, which he had shared with his son and daughter-in-law for some fifteen years. The people living close by suffered from the debilitating effects of rural poverty – most struggled to feed the large number of children they had in their care and many, like Rollinson, had to be content with drawing their domestic water from a nearby pond.

The problems started when Rollinson's son George died unexpectedly on 11 October 1850. In an effort to provide for his wife, George had bequeathed the best of his furniture to Mary, who continued to live in the cottage with her father-in-law. William was distressed by the settlement, as he had hoped his son would leave him the furniture, since he had few other fixtures and fittings to sustain him in his old age. But while Mary continued to live in the cottage and share the furniture with him, this was not a major concern. It was only when another man, Thomas Jermyn, began courting Mary and the two announced plans to wed at Michaelmas in 1851 that Rollinson's resentment began to grow. Initially trying to dissuade her from marrying again before openly declaring his dislike of her fiancé and unwillingness to allow Jermyn to live with them at Sowley Green, Rollinson pushed Mary into declaring her intentions. When she admitted that she would be leaving the cottage after the marriage and taking the furniture with her, the two fell out and the subject became the source of frequent arguments. Rollinson became increasingly detached and sullen and began to formulate more deadly plans to preserve what he thought was his by right.

Mary Rollinson remained blissfully unaware of her father-in-law's intentions, continuing with her preparations for the wedding and doing seasonal agricultural work to make ends meet. On Thursday, 7 August 1851, the old man made the first of a number of attempts to poison the younger woman by mixing a quantity of arsenic into the bag of baking flour she kept in an unlocked trough under the window of the room where she took her meals. Having cooked herself some potatoes and a small dumpling at midday, Mary became increasingly sick and continued to be ill throughout the rest of the afternoon. For several days afterwards she complained of being continually thirsty and having an upset stomach.

A week later she prepared a blackcurrant pudding, using the same poisoned flour that she shared with her niece, Susan Cornell, who had come to visit her from nearby Barnardiston. Both women were taken ill and Susan was forced to return home on Saturday, 16 August. Still without any suspicions of foul play, Mary allowed Susan to take the remains of the blackcurrant pudding back home with her. Over the course of the next few days, Susan's father, a number of her siblings and even some of their neighbours in Barnardiston were taken ill after eating portions of the poisoned pudding. Luckily, they all survived.

Mary Rollinson continued to suffer from the effects of the arsenic poisoning. She remained in bed on Sunday, 17 August, when her sister, Ann Cornell, Susan's mother, arrived to nurse her back to health. On the Monday she was forced to get up and go to work, gleaning in the fields nearby. The following day, still painfully ignorant of the source of her ill-health, Mary baked herself an apple pudding using the noxious flour. Consuming only a small portion of the dish, which she had taken into the fields for her lunch, she was immediately sick and had to sit down and rest on the stubble. She continued to suspect nothing and later that week even passed what remained of the apple pudding to Mrs Jermyn, her future mother-in-law. Five members of the Jermyn family were subsequently poisoned, although each survived the ordeal.

For his part, William Rollinson was conspicuous by his absence during the mealtimes at the cottage. He continued to cook his own food, having a separate bag of flour and refusing anything offered by Mary. For the moment, no one suspected that he lay behind the increasingly frequent bouts of illness afflicting so many of Mary's family and friends.

Another event at this time proved to be a distraction. Desperate for money, William Rollinson had taken in a new lodger. Charlotte Sparkes, a single woman who also took on seasonal work as an agricultural labourer, arrived with her two children, a girl of 11 and a boy of 8. They shared a living room with Mary but had their own separate sleeping area in the cottage. Most importantly, Charlotte had her own cooking provisions and a separate supply of flour.

By Friday, 29 August, Mary Rollinson was still poorly but doing her best to remain active. Charlotte Sparkes and her children had gone away for the weekend and Mary busied herself making some mutton broth using locally bought lamb. The meal produced no ill effects and she saved the bulk of the broth in an iron saucepan which sat on the hob by the side of the fire in the kitchen.

On the Saturday she went to see William Stutter, a doctor at Wickhambrook, some three miles away. Unable to diagnose the reason for her continuing sickness, Stutter administered some leeches, which she was instructed to attach to the side of her body. Requiring the support of her sister in applying the leeches, Mary asked the son of a neighbour to send for Ann Cornell, who duly arrived that evening at around eight o'clock. Both women took supper an hour or so later, eating what remained of the mutton broth that stood on the hob.

Shortly after eating the broth, Ann complained of pains in her head and took to her bed, vomiting throughout the rest of the night. She appeared little better the following morning. Mary suggested that she make some mutton pudding for their dinner, which Ann did later that morning, using the poisoned flour. This was to prove fatal; the pudding poisoned not only Ann but Mary and two of Ann's children who had arrived earlier that day to visit their sick aunt.

Ann was gripped with all of the symptoms of acute arsenic poisoning. As well as experiencing a dryness and metallic taste in her mouth she was racked with severe nausea, colicky abdominal pains and profuse diarrhoea. Accompanying this was a blinding headache, vertigo and muscle cramping. As she began to fade fast on the Sunday afternoon, Thomas Jermyn was sent to get her husband from Barnardiston. The latter arrived at around five o'clock, lifted his wife and children into a horse-drawn cart and took them home. A message was sent to the doctor or 'relieving officer' who was six miles away, but by eight o'clock that evening Ann had slipped away before the medical officer could arrive. While remaining ill, the others made a slow and steady recovery over the coming days and weeks.

At the direction of the local coroner, a post-mortem was

carried out by Mr Stutter, the doctor, on Wednesday, 3 September. The coroner's inquest was held the next day and concluded that Ann Cornell had died of English cholera. Cases of this were not uncommon at the time and the symptoms of the disease could be brought about by drinking unclean pond water. Knowledge of the water supply at Sowley Green must have contributed to the local surgeon's suspicions that this was indeed the cause of death. Ann Cornell was buried in the graveyard at Barnardiston on Friday, 5 September. She left behind a husband and ten children.

Assuming the medical opinions expressed at the coroner's inquest to be correct, Mary Rollinson continued to prepare food using the poisoned flour. A month later, on Thursday, 2 October, she prepared a meal of dumplings and potatoes with Charlotte Sparkes. The two adults ate three of the four dumplings, immediately experiencing a burning sensation in their throats, stomach pains and severe nausea. The two children who had eaten separate dumplings made with Sparkes's uncontaminated supply of flour showed no signs of illness. Alarmed by their condition, the women called a neighbour for help. Strongly suspicious at last that she had been poisoned, Mary gave the remaining fourth dumpling to a dog and a cat outside the cottage. Both were immediately overcome with sickness.

Mr Baker, a surgeon from Great Thurlow, was called in to treat the women. While both were seriously ill, he reported that they should survive their ordeal. He proceeded to send a portion of the vomit from the dog and cat to Mr Deck, a chemist in Cambridge, along with a sample of flour from Mary's bag. The subsequent analysis by the chemist revealed that both samples contained a considerable quantity of arsenic. The discovery of the poison was only possible thanks to the introduction of two important tests for arsenic in the years leading up to the Rollinson murder. These were the Marsh test of 1836 and Riensch test of 1841. Prior to this, tests used by toxicologists had been unreliable and conclusions were often disputed in court.

As a result of Baker's findings, the local police were called in to investigate, led by Superintendent Oliver Death of the West Suffolk Constabulary. A magistrates' inquiry began on Wednesday, 8 October at the *Crown Inn* in Great Thurlow, chaired by the Reverend W Mayd. A warrant was issued against William Rollinson, who was brought before the magistrates and remanded to appear again.

On Saturday, 11 October, a further examination took place at the office of Mr Jardine, the clerk to the magistrates at Haverhill. Benjamin White, a shopkeeper in Great Thurlow, was called in and questioned about the supply of arsenic to William Rollinson. He confirmed that Rollinson had been purchasing small quantities of the poison for many years in order to control rats and mice. Mr Deck, the chemist, reported how he had found the presence of arsenic in both the flour and vomit he had analyzed. When she was called, Charlotte Sparkes told the magistrates that Rollinson had warned her and her children not to eat his daughter-in-law's food for fear of sickness.

Throughout the examination, Rollinson looked drawn and dejected. At the end of the proceedings, he was bailed to appear at Clare Police Station to be further examined on 14 October. As it transpired, he was arrested the very next day on suspicion of the murder of Ann Cornell and locked up at Clare. Despite his acute poverty, the old man was found to have over £11 in his possession and a pocketwatch which was not his own. He failed to explain how he came by these valuables.

With the legal inquiries continuing around them, Mary Rollinson and Thomas Jermyn were finally wed on Monday, 13 October. Mary was still recovering from the effects of the arsenic poisoning but was determined to follow through with her long-planned marriage.

The adjourned magistrates' inquiry resumed at the Station House in Clare the next day. Rollinson was formally charged with administering poison to Mary Rollinson, now Mary Jermyn. The inquiry heard that twenty-four people connected with Mary had been sick as a result of the suspected poisoning. When challenged, Rollinson admitted purchasing arsenic for the purposes of destroying vermin but denied trying to poison anyone. The conduct of Benjamin White in selling him the arsenic was questioned as it became clear that Rollinson had not signed the shop's poison book – a clear violation of the legislation governing the sale of such chemicals. Yet again the proceedings were adjourned.

On Thursday, 16 October, Superintendent Death

*The village of Clare, where William Rollinson was formally charged with
administering poison to his daughter-in-law.*

approached magistrate Reverend Mayd seeking permission to
have the body of Ann Cornell disinterred for examination. The
required order was made and the body was exhumed by police
officers on 18 October. Also present during the unearthing were
the father of the deceased and the doctor, Mr Stutter, who later
removed the intestines from the dead body and sent them to
William Image, a forensic surgeon in Bury St Edmunds.

The magistrates' inquiry was concluded on Monday, 27
October 1851. Rollinson was now being examined on the
twofold charge of murdering Ann Cornwell and attempting to

destroy the life of Mary Jermyn by administering poison. In the light of his age and increasing frailty, the prisoner was allowed to sit at the magistrates' table. He sat throughout the examination with his head resting on his arms, overcome with grief and anxiously watching the evidence unfold.

Superintendent Death testified about the exhumation of Ann Cornell's body and confirmed that the murder charge against Rollinson had come as a result of what the doctors had found. William Image presented the results of his forensic tests, saying, 'I analyzed the tissues of the stomach and detected the presence of arsenic. I next analysed the intestines, and they also contained arsenic, but in much smaller quantities than the stomach. They were inflamed, but little if at all decomposed, which is an important feature in this case.' Asked about the cause of death, he replied, 'The result of the analysis leads me to the opinion that the deceased died from poison and that that poison was arsenic. The fact of the intestines not being decomposed is a strong corroborative proof of the presence of arsenic.'

Benjamin White testified that he had sold Rollinson an ounce of arsenic on 21 or 22 August, but was sketchy about the other occasions he had dispensed poison to the accused. Pressed, he admitted that he had probably served Rollinson on over a dozen other occasions and acknowledged that he had never provided any instructions for administering the arsenic.

When all the evidence had been heard, Rollinson was cautioned and asked if he had anything to say. He replied, 'No, I have nothing to say. I know nothing about it.' The chairman then informed him that it was the magistrates' painful duty to commit him for trial at the next assizes to face both the charges against him. The old man was scarcely able to walk as he was taken away.

Shortly after the magistrates' inquiry another death by poisoning was reported at Great Bradley, less than five miles from Sowley Green. This was a case of a slightly different kind. A coroner's inquest at the *Fox Inn* in the village heard evidence about the demise of 17-year-old Hester Radford, who had passed away earlier that month. She had been 'keeping company' with a young man named Alfred Hines. William Image, the forensic surgeon, reported that a quantity of a well-known plant had been found in the young woman's intestines –

a plant recognized for its use in bringing about abortions. The case served only to highlight the misery caused by the increasing number of poisoning cases occurring in the county at that time.

The 80-year-old William Rollinson faced trial on Thursday, 25 March 1852. The court proceedings began promptly at nine o'clock that morning. Rollinson was 'respectably attired' and, bowing his grey head upon his chest, pleaded nervously 'Not guilty'. He had to be provided with a chair.

Mary Jermyn was the first witness to be called. She described how she and her first husband had shared the cottage at Sowley Green with the accused and testified that her relationship with the older man had become strained after George Rollinson's death. Outlining the friction over the furniture and her

Report on the trial of William Rollinson, 27 March 1852. Ipswich Journal

courtship with Thomas Jermyn, Mary said that William Rollinson had announced one day, 'If you go with Jermyn, you and I must part.' She went on to explain how the first sign of his deep disgruntlement came when he locked her out of the house one Sunday afternoon, requiring her to sleep at a neighbour's. She then outlined the various attempts to poison her from 7 August 1851 and claimed that she was still lame in her feet and legs as a result of the arsenic she had ingested.

The doctors involved in the cases of poisoning were called to testify and repeated the information they had already given at the earlier magistrates' inquiry. Benjamin White also repeated his testimony about selling some arsenic to Rollinson in late August and admitted that a poison book had not been kept in the shop at that time. He claimed not to know about the new legislation requiring this to be done. He also added that he had known Rollinson for some twenty years and had often sold him arsenic for the control of vermin.

At one o'clock, the jury retired for five minutes, during

which time Rollinson asked to leave the court. He was said to be deeply depressed. The judge refused the request. Charlotte Sparkes then testified that before the poisoning incident on 2 October, Rollinson had approached her in the garden of the shared cottage and said, 'If I was you, I would not let my children eat her food.' She believed this was a clumsy attempt by Rollinson to prevent her from eating any food that he had already poisoned for the purposes of murdering Mary Jermyn.

At a quarter past three, after a closing speech by the defence counsel and the judge's summing up, the jury retired to consider its verdict. After a lapse of three minutes, they asked for permission to retire. At ten minutes to five they returned to the court and the foreman delivered a verdict of guilty. He added that they recommended some leniency in sentencing Rollinson on account of his age. Hearing the verdict, Rollinson had to be supported in the dock. He then sank back into his chair and bowed his head in anguish.

In his closing speech, the judge addressed Rollinson by saying, 'You did not intend the death of Ann Cornell, of whose murder you stand convicted, but no doubt you did intend to take away the life of your daughter [in law].' He then indicated that the jury's recommendation for mercy was unlikely to be heard before reflecting that, 'This crime of poisoning has reached a frequency in this and the adjoining county that is altogether appalling, and arsenic is obtained with an ease as if it were one of the common commodities of life. A terrible example must be made to deter others from following so wicked a course.' He then passed the sentence of death on William Rollinson, who had to be assisted from the dock, groaning at his fate, and watched by a great many tearful observers in the courtroom.

Serving only to reinforce the judge's views on the increasing prevalence of poisoning in the county, the next crime facing the court was another tragic case involving arsenic. William Baldry, a 38-year-old farmer 'of respectable appearance' from Preston St Mary, was charged with having administered poison to his wife with intent to murder her. He pleaded 'Not guilty'.

The court heard how the farmer had been in the habit of requesting money from his wife, Mary Ann Baldry. The couple had been married for over ten years and Mary had come into some money a few years before, following the death of her father. When she refused to bow to his constant demands for cash, Baldry had turned nasty and her health began to deteriorate in the latter part of 1851. She had always been a sickly woman, so her symptoms were not spotted immediately. However, acting on the suspicions of her mother, Mrs Harriet Cone – who had removed a sample of water from a glass which Baldry had given to his wife – the police arrested the errant farmer. William Image, the forensic surgeon, analyzed the contents of the small scent bottle presented by Mrs Cone and testified that he had found this to contain a quantity of arsenic sufficient to produce death. When a verdict of guilty was returned by the jury, the judge declared that 'the evidence was clear and overwhelming' and sentenced Baldry to death.

In the aftermath of the trials, there was considerable public opposition to the sentences of death passed against both men. The *Ipswich Journal* reported on Saturday, 3 April 1852 that, 'A petition, numerously signed, has been transmitted from this town [Bury St Edmunds] to Her Majesty's Secretary of State, pleading that the sentences of death against William Rollinson and William Baldry, convicted at the late assizes, may be commuted into transportation.' The same newspaper reported that Rollinson had 'made a confession of his guilt to one of the prisoners', but indicated that, 'we are not aware that this confession has been taken down by the governor of the gaol. He is in a very distressed state of mind'. The sentences of both men were eventually commuted to life imprisonment.

The cases highlighted the popular obsession with poisoning nationally and locally. In the late nineteenth century it became a favourite topic with the press, described by some commentators as a 'fashionable' Victorian crime that had grown out of control. As poisoning could be undertaken in secrecy and its detection relied mainly on circumstantial evidence and the rudimentary, albeit rapidly developing, science of toxicology, it is little wonder that it was perceived to be an easy form of murder. In reality, there was no poisoning epidemic and the number of reported cases of criminal poisoning remained fairly constant throughout the century. And as the case of William Rollinson demonstrated clearly, the criminal justice system was also getting more adept at investigating and prosecuting those who were tempted to misuse the contents of the poison cabinet.

Chapter 8

Murder on the Sabbath

(1853)

'I say no-one else had a hand in the murder but myself.'

When the Reverend Edward Burton Barker heard the church bell of St Mary's ringing on Sunday, 8 May 1853, he knew it was time to leave the rectory for the mile-long walk to deliver his regular Sunday sermon. The 77-year-old Suffolk-born clergyman had officiated at the church in Bacton for more decades than he cared to remember and was well used to hearing the call to prayers. Sarah Percy, a household servant, had already left for the church, and as the Reverend Barker set off at around ten o'clock that morning he left at home the only other resident of the rectory, his trusty and strong-willed housekeeper, Mrs Steggles.

Maria Steggles set about preparing the Sunday lunch, but also found time to open and read her prayer book at regular intervals. She had been the Reverend Barker's housekeeper for well over forty of her sixty-six years and was a diligent and faithful companion to the elderly gentleman. He trusted her with all aspects of the household's management, including the payment of bills and any receipts of money. It was a role she enjoyed and she ran a tight ship.

One of the bell-ringers that day was William Flack, an 18-year-old labourer who lived within a stone's throw of the church. Born in Bacton, the son of Abraham and Ann Flack, William was one of five children, all of whom lived close by. Like many inhabitants of the village, Flack had received no formal education and could neither read nor write. In fact, with a population of around 1,000, the village had not a single school and most families lived in acute poverty. The only form of poor relief was the local workhouse, whose poor institutional practices were noted by Frederich Engels in his 1845 book *The Condition of the Working Class in England*.

Perhaps it was her forthright nature that drove William Flack

The church of St Mary's, Bacton, where the Reverend Edward Burton Barker was rector in 1853.

to dislike Maria Steggles so much. Having been recently dismissed from the Reverend Barker's employment, the young labourer had made no secret of the fact that he bore a grudge against the housekeeper and intended to get even with the clergyman. On one occasion he was overheard proclaiming that he would soon 'steal some of the old parson's mouldy sovereigns'. Only ten days before that particular Sunday, the back door of the rectory had been broken into and a loin of pork and a quantity of eggs stolen. Since that time, the police had been keeping an eye on the premises, although they could not prove that Flack had been involved.

Flack's intentions that Sunday were not clear, although it is most likely that he planned only to rob the rectory. He had already served time for stealing lead from the roof of Bacton Church. Whatever he proposed, his initial plans had an element of deviousness. He later admitted that as a bell-ringer he had 'chimed the parson in', knowing full well that this would leave Mrs Steggles alone at the rectory.

Another bell-ringer that day was Alfred Page, who lodged with Flack. Having rung the bells, both men left the church at around ten-thirty. Page returned home briefly to pick up some letters from their lodgings, and when he emerged, Flack was heading in the direction of the parsonage. Page walked with him for a short time before turning off towards Wyvestone.

According to his later confession, William Flack set about Maria Steggles as soon as he got to the rectory. She came to the back door and Flack pushed his way in. As Steggles backed off into the kitchen, the teenage assailant struck her with his fists and followed up the attack with kicks to her body. The housekeeper fell against the kitchen table, breaking it, and cried out loudly. Her cook's hat flew off and her false hairpiece was wrenched from her head. Flack continued to kick the woman before taking a small knife belonging to his younger brother and cutting her throat in two places. He also struck her on the head with a poker, fracturing her skull, before heading off upstairs to see what he could steal.

Ransacking the rooms, Flack stole a purse and an Elizabethan silver shilling from the room of the servant girl, Sarah Percy. He also took a quantity of money from elsewhere in the house, including three gold sovereigns. By the time he had finished, the haul included a brace of large pistols inscribed with the maker's name, a hunting horn and the poker used to batter the unfortunate Mrs Steggles.

Having left the housekeeper wounded on the floor –

breathing, but fading progressively – Flack headed off down the lane from the rectory, his clothes covered in blood. He paused close to a farm owned by a Mrs Ford to wash his shoes in a ditch before proceeding to hide most of the stolen items in locations close to the village. Having done this he returned to his lodgings to change out of his bloodstained apparel.

Arriving back from the church at twelve-fifteen, the Reverend Barker was greeted with a scene from hell. He and Sarah Percy, the servant girl, approached the rear of the house to find the back door wide open. Entering the kitchen they saw Mrs Steggles lying on her back upon the floor, covered in blood and groaning with pain. The blood from her slashed throat and head wound was sprayed across the floor and around the walls. It even covered the housekeeper's shattered glasses and open prayer book.

Reverend Barker was horrorstruck and left the room. Sarah Percy set off to raise the alarm and returned with three men from the village. One of them ran off to get medical help for the dying Mrs Steggles, and the police were called. When William Cuthbert, a surgeon from Mendlesham, arrived at the scene the housekeeper had passed away. She had survived less than an hour from the time when her employer returned from church.

Combing the house for clues, the police found an unsheathed sword lying on the floor of the parson's room and noted the various items that had been stolen. In the room of the 32-year-old servant girl, they found boxes upturned and a trinket case opened from which money had been taken. A search of the area surrounding the house revealed a trail of footprints running across the clay soil of three or four nearby fields and into a green lane.

An inquest into the death was held on Monday, 9 May. Sarah Percy and the Reverend Barker described how they had attended church the previous day and had returned to find the battered Mrs Steggles on the floor of the kitchen. William Cuthbert outlined the full extent of the injuries that the housekeeper had sustained. The inquest jury returned a verdict of wilful murder by persons unknown.

In the days following the inquest, a reward of £100 was offered by the government for the discovery of the murderer. Still greatly affected by the loss of his trusted housekeeper, the

Reverend Barker offered a further 100 guineas to bring the culprit to justice. The police began questioning one or two suspects, but quickly cleared these of having anything to do with the murder. This included a nephew of Maria Steggles, who was brought into custody and volunteered to go before the local magistrates. He was subsequently found to have been miles away from Bacton at the time of the attack.

Even before his arrest, William Flack was acting oddly and attracting attention. He let slip to one villager that he had not intended to kill Mrs Steggles, but acknowledged that, 'she's dead now, so that's all right'. He purchased some clothes from a Mr Sawyer for 24 shillings and sixpence and at one session of drinking and gaming at the *Shoulder of Mutton Inn* in Old Newton, managed to spend a sum of money equivalent to that stolen from the parsonage. When he then lodged a complaint at the local police station, that he had been robbed of 8 shillings

The Shoulder of Mutton Inn, *Old Newton, where William Flack spent a night drinking and gaming after committing murder.*

and sixpence and his canvas purse had been stolen by a man who was already being held in custody, the police at Bacton were notified.

Inspector Bragg, who was leading the murder investigation, apprehended Flack. The trousers he was wearing appeared to be stained with blood. When questioned about his night at the *Shoulder of Mutton Inn*, the labourer tried to play down the sum he had expended. Unconvinced by the story, Bragg took him into custody, where he was questioned further and charged with murder. A date was set for him to appear before the local magistrates and the police spent the weekend of 21 May searching ditches and ponds in the neighbourhood, although no murder weapon was ever found. A selection of Flack's clothes was sent off to a Professor Taylor of Guy's Hospital in London for forensic examination.

The magistrates' inquiry was held at the *Bull Inn* public

The Bull Inn, *Bacton, scene of the magistrates' inquiry into the death of Maria Steggles.*

house in Bacton, and began on Thursday, 19 May 1853. It attracted much public and media attention. Alfred Page, the bell-ringer, was called to give evidence and described the time he had spent with William Flack on the morning of the murder. He also outlined how he had seen his fellow lodger again that afternoon and had noticed that Flack had changed his clothes. His original clothes were produced as evidence, and the magistrates heard that no blood had been found on them. Flack was questioned, during which he revealed that he had never been to school, did not know his prayers and was not sure whether he was 18 or 19.

On Tuesday, 24 May, Flack was once again brought to the *Bull Inn* from Ipswich Prison. This time the proceedings were held in private, the police having complained that their investigations were being frustrated by the publicity surrounding the case. Inspector Bragg explained how the Elizabethan shilling belonging to the servant girl Sarah Percy had been traced. It had been sold to a Mr Pace, a coin dealer in Bury St Edmunds, for eight pence. Pace often bought old silver, which he smelted down for the bullion content, and the police had found a record of the purchase. When questioned by the magistrates, however, Mr Pace was unable to shed any light on the identity of the person who had sold him the coin.

On the same day, Flack dropped a bombshell. He asked to make a statement and, when permitted to do so, claimed that another person had carried out the crime and he had been paid to keep quiet about it. Orders were given for the person named by Flack to be apprehended and brought before the magistrates. Robert Moore, a local labourer of good character with a wife and four children, accordingly appeared for questioning. He was able to give a good account of himself on the day in question and three other witnesses vouched for his whereabouts at the time of the murder. The magistrates concluded that Moore was not implicated in the murder.

Having removed the prisoner from the room, the magistrates then proceeded to charge William Flack's mother and sister with being accessories to the crime. Ann Flack had admitted destroying her son's shirt on the day after the murder and buying him a new one for ten pence from the shop of Mr Francis in Bacton. Both women were detained in Stowmarket Gaol until 28 May.

At the conclusion of the petty sessions, William Flack was committed for trial at the Summer Assizes in Ipswich. When he appeared before the court in August he pleaded 'not guilty' to the crime and in his statement said: 'Many of the witnesses have sworn falsely. Many of them have sworn part of the truth, and two of them have not said one word of truth. I am an innocent man.' However, the weight of evidence against him was substantial, and having retired for twenty minutes at the conclusion of the trial, the jury returned a verdict of 'guilty'. The trial judge commented that this had been a 'foul and most horrible murder' and condemned the prisoner to be hanged in the grounds of Ipswich Prison on Saturday, 13 August. In receiving the sentence, William Flack appeared unmoved and left the dock with a smile on his face.

In the days following his conviction, Flack once more tried to implicate Robert Moore, asserting that the two of them had gone to the rectory on the morning of the murder. He said that Moore had knocked Maria Steggles down, kicked her in the head and cut her throat, before robbing the house. For his part in the crime, Flack claimed to have taken one of the stolen pistols, a hunting horn and an old shilling. These had been hidden locally. In a fruitless exercise, Mr Alloway, the Governor of Ipswich Prison, went to Bacton and searched for the pistol and hunting horn in the places mentioned by Flack. He found no items to corroborate the prisoner's statement. When Flack's family visited him later that week he was still persisting with the same story.

The date of Flack's execution was eventually deferred since the nominated executioner, William Calcraft, was unable to attend because of other commitments. On Monday, 15 August, Flack had a last visit from his mother, father and sister. It was only at this point that he made a full and honest confession to Mr Alloway. In it he said, 'All I have stated about Moore is false . . . I say no-one else had a hand in the murder but myself.' Having provided some detail on the nature of the crime, Flack ended his confession with a pithy and clearly erroneous assertion: 'I did not hold any spite against Mrs Steggles.' He was hanged within the grounds of the prison on Wednesday, 17 August 1853.

CHAPTER 9

The Maharajah and the Poacher
(1869)

*Rutterford then said he would 'make a clean job of it' and
proceeded to strike the gamekeeper several times . . .*

E riswell, in the west of Suffolk, has a long and colourful history. Close to the site of a Saxon settlement, the village was listed in the Domesday Book of 1086. During the 1700s, Eriswell was owned by the New England Company, which created a number of new thatched and flint-built homes to provide an income for people emigrating to the United States. In 1863, the village was sold to Prince Duleep Singh, the last Sikh Maharajah of the Punjab, who transformed the vast area around his stately home in nearby Elveden into a favoured hunting ground for the Victorian elite. And while this provided much-needed investment for the rapidly declining estate, it also made the open and forested lands a choice habitat for another perennial inhabitant of the Suffolk landscape – the village poacher.

Prince Duleep Singh was born in India in 1838. He was brought to England as a young boy, becoming friends with the British Royal Family, establishing himself within London society and converting to Christianity. Following the death of his mother, he took up residence at Elveden Hall and began the process of developing the Elveden and Eriswell estates for game shooting. It was an interest close to his heart. As a 6-year-old back home in India, the Prince had been educated by two tutors, one to teach him Persian, the court language of his forefathers, and a second to train him in the art of hunting with hawks.

The immensely wealthy Duleep Singh settled into the life of an English country gentleman with apparent ease. He rebuilt the derelict Elveden Hall and set about restoring the village church in Elveden at great cost and to great acclaim. By March 1869, he had also become a magistrate for the West Suffolk area and a respected member of the Suffolk gentry. His estates were stocked with game of all sorts and among the regular visitors to his organized shoots was the Prince of Wales, the future King Edward VII. On one occasion a six-gun hunting party shot a total of 8,312 head of game in a single six-day period on the estate.

All this required a large staff, and Duleep Singh employed experienced men to manage his estates and protect the large number of grouse, pheasants and partridges raised especially for his shooting parties. One of these was gamekeeper John Hight, a 19-year-old man well known to the small fraternity of local poachers who took their chances in illegally trapping and shooting game on the estate. Always carrying a stick and wearing his characteristic sealskin cap, Hight was also well known and well liked in the small community around Eriswell.

There continued to be tough penalties at this time for those found guilty of poaching, although the crime was endemic in many parts of Suffolk. The Black Act of 1723 had made poaching with a blackened face a capital offence for which hanging became the established punishment. Just being caught in possession of poaching equipment could often result in a year in prison or, at worst, transportation, all of which made the night-time activities of the poachers a deadly serious pursuit, as John Hight was to discover to his cost in the early evening of Friday, 31 December 1869.

That afternoon, two local men, 27-year-old James Rutterford and 21-year-old David Heffer, had ventured onto the Eriswell estate with a shotgun in pursuit of game which they planned to sell the next day in Mildenhall. Having bagged some birds for their illicit trade on a part of the estate known as the Crinkle Crankle belt, the poachers were heading for home through some woodland when they were heard and pursued by gamekeeper Hight. In the course of the chase, Heffer dropped his cap and as he stooped to pick it up was caught by Hight, who held him firmly.

Rutterford ran back to help his colleague and challenged Hight to let Heffer go, striking the gamekeeper on the arm with the shotgun he carried. Both men recognized each other. Hight then backed away, but Rutterford lunged at him again, bringing the firearm down on Hight's head and flooring him instantly. Heffer shouted for them both to run, but Rutterford was fearful of the consequences of being caught for poaching, having seriously assaulted Hight. Announcing that he would rather risk the noose than be transported, Rutterford then said he would 'make a clean job of it' and proceeded to strike the gamekeeper several times with both the barrel and the breech of the gun until he was dead. He then dragged the body off to hide it elsewhere in the woods before both men headed for home at around twenty minutes to seven.

The evening was cold and wet, and on their way back to the village the two poachers experienced more bad luck. They ran into Police Constable Charles Peck, who stopped them, suspecting that they had been up to no good. Peck was stationed at Icklingham and happened to be on duty at the turnpike on the Mildenhall to Thetford road. Having seen some movement in the darkness, he had watched both men emerge from a nearby turnip field on to the road. He had, in fact, spoken to the pair earlier that evening on the same road and had suspected that they might be out poaching. David Heffer immediately ran off carrying the bagged game birds, but PC Peck was able to wrestle the loaded, double-barrelled, shotgun from Rutterford and asked him to turn out his pockets.

Rutterford was found to be carrying the sealskin cap he had taken from the dead gamekeeper. When asked why he had this in his possession, Rutterford claimed that it was 'a spare'. Suspicious, but unable to prove it was stolen, Peck allowed the poacher to make his way home with the cap, but retained the shotgun for further investigation. It was to prove a wise move.

A search party was organized the next day when it was clear that Hight had failed to return home from his woodland patrol. His body was soon found, partially covered and hidden within a gorse thicket. His stick was discovered nearby but it was noted that his hat was missing. The body was taken to the *Chequers Inn* in Eriswell, a public house that often served as a local mortuary at that time. A post-mortem revealed that he had died as a result of several blows to the head.

Rutterford and Heffer were immediately arrested for the crime. PC Peck took the shotgun he had wrestled from Rutterford and presented it to John Allen, a gamekeeper on a neighbouring estate. When examined, the barrel was found to be twisted and dented, supporting the theory that it had been used to batter the unfortunate gamekeeper. Some shot was also found to be jammed in the barrel of the gun. It later transpired

The Chequers Inn, *Eriswell, where the coroner's inquest into the death of gamekeeper John Hight began in January 1870.*

that this matched some unused shot found close to Hight's body. Human hair was also discovered on the ramrod and stock of the gun where the ramrod was inserted. This was retained for later analysis by a local surgeon.

An inquest into the death of the gamekeeper was held at the *Chequers Inn* during January 1870. Leading the inquiry was none other than Magistrate Duleep Singh. Both Rutterford and Heffer were invited to testify at the inquest. In his testimony, Heffer already began to give the first hints that he wished to distance himself from the crime. The jury had no hesitation in returning a verdict of 'wilful murder' against both men. The pair were committed for trial at the Suffolk Assizes in March 1870.

The crime became a talking-point within the small, tight-knit community around Eriswell and was sensationalized in the national press. Local people showed little support or sympathy for the accused, and most were horrified by the murder. In fact, there were echoes of a case some eighteen years earlier when William Napthen, a gamekeeper at Elveden, was shot and murdered while chasing six poachers on an estate belonging to a Mr Newton. While three of the accused eventually stood trial for the crime at the Lent Assizes in Ipswich in April 1851, all had been found 'not guilty', since it had not been possible to prove beyond reasonable doubt that the men were those identified as being on the estate at the time of the murder. Even the lesser charge of poaching was dropped because of a similar lack of evidence.

In the weeks that followed, Hight's bloody cap was found hidden in a muddy bank on the road towards Mildenhall – the route taken by Rutterford after he had been detained by PC Peck on the night of the murder. An earlier search of Rutterford's home had also revealed traces of blood on some of the poacher's clothes, even though they appeared to have been washed. Rutterford's own behaviour did little to convince the authorities that he might be innocent – in the lead-up to his trial he made an unsuccessful attempt to escape from gaol.

The trial in March proved to be both shocking and enlightening. The trial judge, Mr Justice Byles, announced to the jury at the start of the proceedings that David Heffer had made an application to the court to give evidence on the part of the Crown (what we would now call turning Queen's evidence). The judge provided a suitable caveat however: 'If Heffer were present, aiding and abetting or consenting in any way, he is guilty, and if he did not disclose his knowledge as soon as he ought to have done he would be guilty of misprision of felony, at the very least.' A dozen witnesses were called to support the assertion that Heffer played no part in the killing and in the light of this information the charges against him were dropped. His evidence as a witness proved to be both insightful and damning in the case against Rutterford.

Heffer went on to provide details of how the two men had entered the woods for the purposes of poaching. He admitted that the shotgun used had been his, but stated clearly that it was Rutterford who had used it to kill both the pheasants and John Hight. He described their encounter with the gamekeeper and Rutterford's savage attack on the man, including his desire to make a 'clean job' of it. He also confirmed that prior to the murder Hight had said he knew Rutterford, and the latter had made it clear that he knew the gamekeeper.

The case was a landmark for forensic science. It was the first time that a murder case in the county had involved the comparison of human hairs taken from a crime scene. The hairs found on the shotgun taken by PC Peck from Rutterford on the night of the murder proved to be invaluable evidence when it was found that these matched hairs from the dead gamekeeper.

There was clear evidence of Rutterford's intention to cover up the crime. One witness described how he had found the body of the murdered gamekeeper:

He was lying a little on his side, with his arms extended over his head. Some furze and a velvet frock were covered over him. Some of the furze that covered him was growing there and some of it was cut. This shows it must have been a deliberate act, this covering the body.

Heffer's testimony was both pivotal and galling. Under examination, he admitted running away from PC Peck when stopped on the night of the murder. His actions the following day also suggested that he had few scruples. He travelled to Mildenhall to sell one of the pheasants taken the previous evening and spent some time drinking in the *Prince of Wales* public house before calling on Rutterford.

In the light of the overwhelming case against him, it came as no surprise that Rutterford was duly convicted of murder and sentenced to death. But in what might be poetically described as Suffolk's own story of 'the man they couldn't hang', Rutterford, like Heffer, was to escape the noose. Much to the chagrin of the local population, James Rutterford received a last-minute reprieve. With only thirty-six hours to go before his planned execution, the poacher's sentence was commuted to one of penal servitude for life.

The decision not to proceed with the hanging resulted from a technicality, what *The Times* described on Saturday, 9 April 1870 as the 'difficulty in executing the sentence of the law without risk of failure'. Owing to some scarring on Rutterford's face and throat, the result of a severe burn earlier in his life, it was felt that it would be 'unsafe' to hang the condemned man by ordinary means for fear of prolonging his suffering.

As it turned out, Rutterford died within three years as an inmate of Pentonville Prison in London. The prison was designed to hold over 500 inmates under the 'separate system', with each prisoner having his own cell, thirteen feet long, seven feet wide and nine feet high. Had he survived, Rutterford would have spent his remaining days undertaking repetitive manual work like weaving or unpicking tarred rope. Pentonville was to become the model for all British prisons in the years that followed, with a further fifty-four being built to the same design over the course of the next six years.

David Heffer fared little better. Having been forced to leave his home county after the trial, he eventually returned to Suffolk in 1885, employed as a worker on the Fordham–Mildenhall railway. He died the same year, his death the result of a broken blood vessel.

Rutterford became infamous as a poacher and a murderer, his exploits sensationalized in a nineteenth-century ballad entitled 'The Trial and Condemnation of James Rutterford'. The case serves only to highlight the absurdity of the existing laws governing poaching, which turned many country folk into hardened criminals for pilfering a small amount of game while rich landowners continued to slaughter excessive quantities of wildlife as a legitimate country pursuit.

There is one other postscript to this tale which is worthy of mention. As the architect of the game preserve on which John Hight was so brutally killed, Maharajah Duleep Singh would himself face an ignominious end. In 1886 he underwent a conversion back to Sikhism and sought to return to his homeland to reclaim his position as leader of the Sikh people. Travelling as far as Aden, he was arrested by the British authorities and forced to return to Europe. He then began a secret and ultimately unsuccessful campaign to build support for a Sikh uprising against British colonial oppression. However, his health was to fail him, and while staying at the Hotel de la Tremouille in Paris in October 1893 he suffered a fatal epileptic fit. He was eventually buried in a simple grave within the churchyard at Elveden and remembered as a popular and enigmatic Suffolk resident.

Gravestone of the Maharajah Duleep Singh, once a West Suffolk magistrate, who owned the Eriswell estate and chaired the inquest into the death of John Hight, his gamekeeper employee.

CHAPTER 10

A Death at the *Ship Inn*

(1880)

Rattled, he snapped, 'Go you to your sherry bottle – that's what you like best.'

The Suffolk market town of Beccles stands on a hill above the marshes of the River Waveney, close to the border with Norfolk. In the latter part of the nineteenth century there was only one road bridge crossing the river from the Norfolk side, and this lay beside the *Ship Inn*, a public house that received its fair share of custom from the millers, maltsters, farmers and woodmen that passed by in the course of their daily business. With a population fast approaching 6,000, Beccles retained the feel of a small, close-knit community, where anything out of the ordinary was quick to become the focus of town gossip. Events at the *Ship Inn* on the evening of Tuesday, 12 October 1880 would set those tongues wagging and see the landlord of the public house tried

An early photograph of the Ship Inn, *Beccles, some thirty years after it was run by James and Sarah Flowers.*

for the murder of his 67-year-old wife, Sarah Ann Flowers.

James Nelson Flowers liked a drink. No one sought to deny that. The 53-year-old innkeeper was well known for indulging his thirst, often with serious consequences. In March 1867 he was found guilty of being drunk and disorderly in Smallgate, and the Beccles Police Court fined him 5 shillings for his intoxication. In November 1873 he was charged with assaulting James Nelson, a fellow innkeeper, although the case was subsequently dismissed. Not that his wife could complain too much, as she was equally addicted to the bottle and regularly spent her evenings getting slowly more inebriated and occasionally falling over. And while most regulars at the inn felt that the couple rubbed along nicely, a few would later testify that James Flowers had been known to hit his wife during their occasional domestic spats.

Sarah Flowers appeared to be well down the road of being drunk by the lunchtime of the day in question. Her husband later claimed that he had 'begged her not to drink', but his words seem to have fallen on deaf ears. Alfred Francis, an engine driver in a nearby wood yard and a next-door neighbour to the Flowers, called at the inn around midday. He found the landlady inebriated and in a tetchy mood. As he was enjoying a pint in the taproom, James Flowers was explaining to him that he had sprained his wrist. Sarah called across to her husband and remonstrated with her fist, 'Yes, and it is a damn pity you can't sprain the other. Then you wouldn't knock me about as you do.' The publican retorted dryly, 'Go you along, you drunken old sod.'

When Arthur Peck, a sawyer from Ringsfield, arrived for his lunch at about one o'clock the tetchiness of the landlady was still evident. As she served Peck with a beer, she told James in no uncertain terms that his dinner was ready, to which he replied, somewhat curtly, 'I'll come in a minute or two.' Some twenty minutes later, as James continued to talk to his customers, she appeared again with the same information. Rattled, he snapped, 'Go you to your sherry bottle – that's what you like best.'

A steady flow of customers appeared throughout the afternoon. Herbert Webb, a maltster from Gillingham, called in for a drink at four-fifteen. He was served by the intoxicated landlady, who could still walk but was having to steady herself on a nearby settle. When James came in from the stable with another customer, he too appeared to be the worse for wear, and in response to an offhand remark from his wife that he should 'go after his old whores', merely put his hand up to his mouth and made a jeering noise.

When regulars William Goodman and Alexander Ward entered the taproom some fifteen minutes later, the drunken behaviour continued. In response to Goodman's enquiry about her health, Sarah waved her hand flamboyantly and answered him by declaring, 'I'm middling, thank you,' while continuing to cling on to the settle for support. Having seen her in this state many times before, neither man was unduly perturbed. Ward was then shown the landlord's sprained wrist and when he suggested that Mrs Flowers should bathe it in some hot water, Sarah came across and placed her hand on her husband's arm saying, rather obscurely, 'Good bye child, good bye dear.' By this time James was ignoring her frequent interjections.

Thirteen-year-old Emily Rose Bird, known to the couple as 'Rosa,' then appeared in the bar to pick up a half pint of stout for her father, Benjamin Bird. She saw Goodman and Ward in the taproom, although both men left shortly afterwards. Mrs Flowers was still clinging on to the settle, but both she and James came into the bar to serve the girl. James picked up a mug for the stout and offered it to his wife who usually attended to Rosa's needs. Sarah ignored her husband's outstretched arm and picked up a different mug before shuffling off to the beer cellar, a small room off the main bar. Negotiating the four-inch step down from the bar into the cellar, she stooped to draw the mug of stout. But as she tried to stand up the landlady fell backwards onto the brick floor of the cellar and cried out a number of times, 'Oh! Dear Rosa, come and pick me up.' Seemingly unconcerned for his wife's welfare, James called out from the taproom that he didn't think Rosa would be able to lift her, to which Sarah replied, 'Child, come and try.'

Entering the room, Rosa did her best to lift the older woman. She managed to drag the landlady across the floor to leave her lying on her right side with her head close to the cellar door and her legs across the threshold. The youngster remained close to her, unsure what to do next. Still showing no concern, James came into the cellar and seeing the stout spilt on the floor went

Ship Inn, *Beccles, now a private home, but once a public house run by James and Sarah Flowers.*

off to fetch a cloth. Having found one he decided to remain in the taproom and sat down. Out of earshot, Sarah said to Rosa, 'Oh, that old varmint has knocked me down.' Confused, Rosa replied, 'No Mrs Flowers, he did not, you fell down.' Seeing that James had no intention of coming to her aid, Sarah then called out, 'I will have you taken away before the end of the night,' to which her husband responded, 'And I will have you, you drunken old beast. You was drunk in the morning at ten or eleven o'clock.'

By this stage the public house was empty of other customers. Rosa asked James if he could get her the mug of stout. He came through to do so and stepped over his wife. Sarah exclaimed that Rosa should have neither the mug nor the beer and repeatedly swore at the girl. James ignored the protestations and filled the mug for Rosa. He then asked her if she would help to clean the floor of the cellar which Rosa, anxious to get away, said she could not do. She left the couple alone shortly afterwards.

Maltster William Shelgrave was the next to arrive at the inn at around twenty minutes to six. He did not see Sarah Flowers, but could hear her groaning as she still lay on the floor of the cellar. He assumed she was pained by what he later described as her 'rheumatics'. Alice Francis, the 11-year-old daughter of neighbour Alfred Francis, arrived not long afterwards. She had called in to pick up the key to their house, which her father had left at the bar that lunchtime. Passing the taproom, she saw the landlord and Shelgrave talking over a beer and was then astonished to see the body of Sarah Flowers in the cellar. Initially she could see only the landlady's feet lying close to the doorway, but as she approached the room was concerned to see Mrs Flowers, lying face down on the brick floor, alive but incapacitated. Frightened, she cried out before running off to get help from Hannah Willingham, a servant girl who worked for her father.

Hannah Willingham, who lodged with the Francis family, came to the inn having heard Alice's story. The timing of this remains unclear – when questioned later she recalled it was 'about six o'clock' by the timepiece at the inn, but was not sure that this was accurate. However, William Shelgrave did recall seeing her enter the inn, so we can assume that this must have been sometime after twenty to six. James met her at the front door and announced, 'Hannah, go in, my wife lays drunk in the cellar.' Willingham then walked through to find Sarah comatose on the floor. At James's request, she did her best to lift Sarah, placing her arms around the older woman's waist and dragging her sideways out of the cellar and into the main bar area. Sarah had apparently moved her legs at this point and with some difficulty Willingham managed to support and manoeuvre her onto a chair at the bar. As she was being moved James said something to his wife which Willingham failed to hear, prompting Sarah to say, 'Believe him, believe him.'

The 19-year-old domestic servant knew the couple well, having worked for them on a number of occasions. She was also well used to seeing Mrs Flowers drunk and later described how she had known her to fall over and injure herself on more than one occasion. As such, she was not immediately concerned for

Sarah's safety. Having left her perched on the chair, she went upstairs with James to make up a bed for the landlady.

In her later testimony, Willingham described how she had come back downstairs to find Sarah still sitting in the chair, but with her head tilted right back and her eyes and mouth wide open. She also claimed that the landlady had not spoken. Crucially, she would also testify that she had left the inn to get help, fearing that the woman was dead at this point. As we will see later, her version of events proved to be inconsistent in a number of respects.

John Finch, a groom in a nearby wood yard, called at the inn around five minutes past six. Sitting in the taproom with the landlord, he heard a noise in the bar, which he later described as being similar to the 'groaning' he had heard Mrs Flowers make on previous occasions. James Flowers, still showing every sign of being inebriated, announced: 'My old woman has been drinking again; she is a high mettled old woman and will have her own way.' Alfred Francis, the neighbour, returned to the taproom just after this, while Finch was still talking to the landlord. He later claimed that his son had given him a message from James asking him to go to the inn, and said that while in the taproom he had not seen Mrs Flowers. He also claimed that the door to the bar was closed at that time, which would have prevented him from seeing the chair on which Sarah was sitting. When Francis then left, only John Finch remained in the taproom, and when he departed a short while later, James Flowers took the unusual step of locking the doors and closing the inn for the evening. Ordinarily, the inn would not close before eleven o'clock at night.

Whether Sarah Flowers was dead or dying at this juncture we may never know, and the evidence presented at the trial did little to pinpoint with any accuracy the timing of her demise. What is clear is that Hannah Willingham returned to the inn at around six-thirty that evening, accompanied by Harriet Beane, a charwoman in the town. The latter had worked for Mrs Flowers for some eleven years and also knew about her drunken exploits. To their surprise, they found the inn in darkness and the doors locked. Rattling the shutters on the windows they eventually roused James Flowers, who looked out from an upstairs window and angrily announced that his wife was in bed. This was in fact a lie – dead or alive, Sarah had not left the bar. Having departed, Beane returned on her own at around eight o'clock that evening, still concerned about Sarah's health. This time she was unable to get any response from the household.

Alfred Francis rose early the next morning and called at the inn around ten to six as he was in the habit of doing. He found James drawing up a blind and called out to him, 'Oh, you don't want calling this morning; you are up.' The landlord failed to respond, but as the engine driver went to walk off, he heard his neighbour call after him: 'There's a rare bad job happened,' he announced, before going on to say, 'The poor old girl is dead and is lying here in the bar.' Following James into the house, Francis could see the body of Mrs Flowers on the floor. She appeared to have fallen from the chair at the bar. He took hold of her hand and immediately recognized that she had been dead for some time. Telling James to leave the body exactly where it was and not to 'meddle with her', he then sent his children for the police and the doctor.

Mr Edward Bowles Crowfoot, the surgeon, was called to the scene just after seven o'clock on the morning of Wednesday, 13 October. Arriving at the inn he found the body of Mrs Flowers on the floor of the bar. He concluded that she had been dead for some hours. While he found a few bruises on her face and body, he could see no immediate signs of the cause of death. This would only be revealed by his later post-mortem, which showed that Sarah Flowers had sustained a number of injuries to her body, including ten broken ribs on the left side of her chest and eight on the right. Crowfoot concluded that she had died as a result of the shock to her system caused by these injuries. Furthermore, he believed that these broken bones could not have been accidentally inflicted, but must have been caused by some other person jumping or kneeling upon the breastbone. As it appeared that only James Flowers was with his wife at the time of death, he was held to be the prime suspect and was duly arrested and taken to Beccles Police Station on Gaol Lane for questioning.

An inquest was held before County Coroner C W Chaston over the course of the next two days. The chief constable and deputy chief constable both attended the hearing, which was already generating considerable interest from the press and local population. Mr F J Dowsett was appointed to represent the prisoner and sat through the inquest proceedings.

A number of witnesses were called to testify on the events leading to Sarah Flowers's death. These were Alfred and Alice Francis, John Finch, Hannah Willingham and Harriet Beane. Charlotte Mills, the wife of a local waterman and an acquaintance of the Flowers, also testified that the landlady had, at different times, complained about James beating her. She recollected one morning just before harvest time, when Mrs Flowers had come to her house and asked if her friend would take her in and look after her, announcing that she was afraid to return to the inn. When they both returned to the *Ship Inn* she found that James did not seem very angry, although it was clear that they had been quarrelling.

Two married women, Mary Ann Ward and Sarah Ward, gave evidence about Sarah Flowers's drinking habits, but also claimed to have heard cries of 'murder' about ten o'clock on the Tuesday night. Sarah Ward went on to say that she had been reluctant to disclose this to the police during their investigations as she believed the cries were made by an 'invalid lady' who lived close by, and was 'out of her mind'.

Surgeon Edward Crowfoot presented the conclusions of his post-mortem examination, emphasizing that the injuries to Mrs Flowers had not been the result of an accident. The working hypothesis at this stage was that Sarah had died during the night, rather than in the early evening. Having heard two days of testimony, the coroner's jury took thirty minutes to return a verdict of 'wilful murder' against James Flowers. By order of the coroner, Sarah's body was buried in Beccles Cemetery on Saturday, 16 October 1880. She was recorded as being a 'nonconformist'.

The local magistrates wasted no time in hearing the case against the publican. The proceedings at the police court in Beccles opened on the same day that Sarah Flowers was buried. Mr F J Dowsett represented the prisoner. The first day of the proceedings saw a repeat of many of the testimonies given at the coroner's inquest. While generally reiterating the story she had given there, aspects of Hannah Willingham's evidence did not appear to be consistent with her earlier testimony. In front of the magistrates, she first claimed – as she had testified earlier – that she had fetched Mrs Beane, the charwoman, because she thought 'Mrs Flowers required help'. Questioned a second time, she said that she thought Mrs Flowers 'was dead' when she left her.

There also appeared to be some discrepancy about whether Willingham had entered the inn alone at that time. Alice Francis told the magistrates that having seen Mrs Flowers lying on the floor of the cellar she had been frightened and had left to find Willingham. She then described how she had returned with the domestic servant at a quarter past six – another inconsistency – and watched her pick up Mrs Flowers. Hannah Willingham had not mentioned at the coroner's inquest that Alice had accompanied her. Re-called to give evidence during the resumption of the court on Tuesday, 19 October, Willingham backed up Alice's testimony by stating that the pair had gone to the inn together that evening.

William Shelgrave, one of the later witnesses, also supported the notion that the two girls had been together. He told the magistrates that he saw Willingham go into the cellar, but claimed that the girls just looked in and left again by the front door. All three would later change their stories.

Hannah Willingham's testimony proved to be crucial to the conduct of the inquiry.

Report on the death of Sarah Flowers. Lowestoft Journal

THE SUPPOSED WIFE MURDER AT BECCLES.

The coroner's inquest had pursued the theory that whatever violence had been inflicted on Sarah Flowers, this had occurred at night. The prosecution held that Willingham's evidence made this assumption untenable and argued that the landlady was dead by six o'clock. Adopting this as probable, the surgeon, Edward Crowfoot, gave evidence that it was quite possible that the woman could have been dragged from the cellar to the chair on which she was sat, to die almost immediately in an upright position. However, he went on to state his belief that the injury to Mrs Flowers's ribs was sustained *before* she was moved and she had later fallen off the chair and died on the floor.

When all the evidence had been presented, Mr Dowsett indicated that he had advised his client to reserve his defence entirely. This was principally because the prosecution had suggested a different time of death to that assumed by the coroner's inquest. Having been duly cautioned, James Flowers was invited to speak. He said that he had urged his wife not to drink that day but she had been drunk that morning and had fallen down a number of times throughout the day. Mr R Dashwood, the chairman of the magistrates, then said that Flowers would be committed for trial and should reserve anything else he had to say. The prisoner responded by saying, 'I hadn't an angry word with her at all. She has been going on in this way for years and years – drunk day after day ... I am innocent of that, so help me God ... '

James Flowers's trial took place at the Suffolk Assizes in November 1880. Leading the prosecution was Mr Gates QC, with Mr Simms Reeve defending the prisoner. When asked how he wished to plead, Flowers said 'Not guilty' in a firm, clear voice. The *Lowestoft Journal* reported later that he 'appeared perfectly calm and collected'.

Entrance to Beccles Gaol where James Flowers was held in 1880.

In opening the case for the prosecution, Mr Gates asked the jury to lay aside any opinions they had formed about the case based on what they might have read in the press. In his view the case against the prisoner was one of purely circumstantial evidence, but the injuries that had led to Sarah Flowers's death could not have been self-inflicted or the result of an accident. He aimed to show that the death resulted from external violence and that James Flowers was the only person who could have committed such an act. He believed that the landlady's death was the result of a quarrel between man and wife, exacerbated by Sarah Flowers's drunkenness. In conclusion, he said that if he proved this, and the jury believed that the woman had provoked her husband to strike her in anger, it would be perfectly open for them to reach a verdict of manslaughter.

The early witnesses in the trial gave evidence about the events throughout the lunchtime and early afternoon of Tuesday, 12 October. Arthur Peck, Herbert Webb, William Goodman and Alexander Ward recounted seeing the couple drunk and being tetchy with each other. Emily Rose Bird explained how she had seen Mrs Flowers fall backwards in the cellar and had tried unsuccessfully to pick her up off the brick floor.

Alice Francis was called to testify how she had gone to the *Ship Inn* to get the key to her house, had seen Mrs Flowers lying on the floor of the cellar and had gone home to tell Hannah Willingham what she had witnessed. Accounts of the trial show her evidence to be muddled. At first she maintained that she returned to the inn with Willingham and went into the house. Later she admitted that while she told the magistrates she had returned to the inn with Willingham, the latter had in fact gone to pick up the deceased woman on her own.

Despite their earlier statements, Hannah Willingham and William Shelgrave also made no further reference to Alice Francis returning to the inn. Shelgrave merely stated that he saw Willingham come into the public house and heard the landlord ask her to pick up his wife who was lying on the floor of the cellar. Willingham gave every indication that she had acted alone and was not challenged on this point.

Her testimony also raised another concern. During the coroner's inquest she said that she had sought assistance from Mrs Beane because she thought 'Mrs Flowers required help'. At the magistrates' court she appeared to change tack on this by admitting that she thought Mrs Flowers 'was dead' by the time she left her. When cross-examined on this point, she stuck to this assertion. When Mr Reeve asked, 'Did you think she was dead then?' Willingham answered, 'Yes, I did.' Reeve challenged her again, 'Do you still think she was dead then?' 'Yes,' she replied, 'I do. I believe she was dead when I left the house.'

This apparent concern for Mrs Flowers's welfare does not sit well with other strands of Willingham's testimony given at the magistrates' court. During those proceedings she admitted that having left the inn to get some assistance from Mrs Beane, she stopped in at her employer's house to make some tea for Mr Francis and suggested that this took about ten minutes. Are we really to believe that this was the action of a person who believed that the landlady was dead or dying?

Similarly, when she had returned to the inn with Harriet Beane and the pair had failed to gain access to the premises, Willingham, it seems, took no further action. And while the charwoman did make one further attempt to find out if Sarah Flowers was in any danger, neither woman attempted to raise the alarm or call the police to the scene. For someone who was so convinced of the landlady's demise, this seems to be odd behaviour.

Alfred Francis's evidence also appeared to be somewhat inconsistent with his earlier statements. Having gone to the inn at lunchtime and again at around four o'clock that afternoon, he testified at the trial that he had returned to the inn at ten minutes past six. At the magistrates' court he had given the time as both 'five minutes to six' and 'six o'clock'. He also gave no explanation as to why he had gone to the inn for a third time that day. In his earlier statement he claimed that it was on account of what his young son came to tell him. Could it be that his son had relayed Hannah Willingham's concerns while delivering the tea to his father?

Francis also played down suggestions that the couple had bickered on a regular basis. He admitted that he had known them to 'have words together', but said he had never known them to come to blows and believed 'they were not quarrelsome people'. This was not quite the picture painted by Charlotte Mills and Harriet Beane, who had both testified earlier that the couple often argued and James Flowers had been seen to strike his wife on at least one occasion.

Surgeon Edward Crowfoot expanded on the medical evidence he had given at the two previous inquiries, explaining that the post-mortem examination had identified small, newly formed, bruises on the ribs, thigh, leg and elbow of the deceased. The broken ribs had also penetrated the pleura and he had found a small quantity of blood on both sides of the ribcage. Sarah Flowers's heart had also showed signs of fatty degeneration and, when cross-examined, Crowfoot said that from what he had observed, he believed the woman to have been 'a confirmed drunkard'.

He speculated that the broken ribs had resulted from someone jumping or kneeling on the chest of the deceased or from falling from a great height. However, he went on to say that while 'It was quite possible for a person to fall a short distance and break two or three ribs . . . it was impossible to break eighteen ribs in this way,' and added, 'The fact that the floating or unattached ribs were fractured would indicate more than an application of force.'

The examination of the skull had revealed some serous fluid between the *dura mater* and the surface of the brain, and Crowfoot admitted that it was possible that this had caused death. He also suggested that this would have rendered the landlady insensible to pain, explaining why she had not cried out when lifted from the floor by Hannah Willingham. He concluded that death had resulted from either a fit of serous apoplexy or the shock caused by the injuries to her ribs. In his earlier testimony, he had already suggested that 'The anaemic condition of the brain, the pale and healthy appearance of the lungs, and the emptiness of the right side of the heart, all pointed to sudden death.'

Mr W Cadge, a Norwich surgeon, was called to the stand to comment on Crowfoot's evidence. He concurred with his surgeon colleague's interpretation, adding, 'The fracture of the eighteen ribs must have been caused by some indirect pressure on the breastbone, and direct violence on the ribs themselves. In all probability a person having sustained such an injury would be in a state of collapse,' and added that he would, 'not expect to find external marks of violence in a case of broken ribs. It was not often that when a person lived there were outward bruises when ribs were broken; when a person died it was still less likely there would be bruises.'

In his summing up for the defence, Simms Reeve pointed out that the Flowers were addicted to drink and while occasionally bickering, were not a quarrelsome couple. On only one occasion had James Flowers been seen to raise a hand to his wife. He then reminded the jury that they could not find the prisoner guilty of murder unless they were satisfied that the cause of death was due to the acts of the prisoner himself. In any case, what motive did the landlord have for killing his wife? And, if he, or someone else, had injured her, why was nothing heard in the street? He went on to suggest that the injuries were accidentally inflicted and maintained that the prosecution had more or less admitted that no jury would find the prisoner guilty of murder on the basis of the evidence presented. He argued, therefore, that the jury had only to consider the crime of manslaughter and contended that it would even be difficult to find him guilty of that.

The trial judge echoed a number of these points, repeating that the jury had to decide beyond all reasonable doubt whether the prisoner was guilty of murder or manslaughter. He pointed out that while they were heavy drinkers, there was no evidence to justify the jury coming to the conclusion that James Flowers had habitually and brutally ill-treated his wife and went on to say that there was also no evidence of provocation, squabbling, bad feeling, fighting or scuffling. The key question for the jury was whether the evidence showed that the landlord was guilty of an act of violence towards his wife that had resulted in her death. Mere suspicion would not do.

After an absence of only five minutes, the jury returned with its verdict – 'not guilty'. James Flowers walked free, to the surprise of many local people. He would only live another eight years himself, passing away in 1888. He was buried on Monday, 16 April, in the same cemetery as his wife. Having given up running a public house, his profession was recorded as that of a 'hay dealer'.

CHAPTER 11

A Case of Common Practice
(1880)

When the father checked on the condition of his son at around
three o'clock that afternoon, he found the boy in the last throes
of death . . .

Child cruelty can take many forms and has always
been a challenging area for lawmakers and criminal
justice agencies. In the nineteenth century it was
particularly difficult to criminalize such behaviour
when many of the underlying public attitudes towards the care
and control of children were at best authoritarian and at worse
barbaric. Despite this, there were always singular and repellent
examples that shocked public morality and furthered the case
for reform. And Suffolk, like other counties, experienced its fair
share of these malevolent offences against children throughout
the period.

An early example was the murder of 8-year-old Mary Ann
Smith in Cookley, near Halesworth, in the winter of 1812.
Husband and wife John and Elizabeth Smith were hanged for
the crime in Ipswich on 23 March, to the satisfaction of the
many thousands who had gathered for the spectacle. Mary Ann
was the eldest of John's three offspring. When his first wife died
he remarried and Elizabeth became an unwilling stepmother to
the children. With John ignoring her increasingly vindictive
treatment, Elizabeth subjected the infants to a regime of terror
that included starvation, locking them up in outbuildings in the
depths of winter and hanging them up by ropes. Mary Ann was
raised up by a rope around her middle and left to hang, dying
eventually of starvation and deprivation. The jury took just five
minutes to find the couple 'guilty'.

No less shocking was the case of Joseph Clark, a 13-year-old
farm worker, who died from the kicks he received from his hot-
headed and dictatorial master, Simon Quy Viall, of Middleton
Hall, near Sudbury, in December 1844. Charged with

manslaughter, the farm owner was eventually found 'not guilty' in a case that aroused considerable revulsion amongst the people of Sudbury.

Sudbury was also to play host to a startling example of child cruelty which again involved the hanging of a child. William Bear, a 33-year-old silk weaver, lived with his large but impoverished family in Globe Passage, off New Street, in Sudbury. His 10-year-old son, also called William, had a reputation as a young tearaway and was later described as being 'addicted to pilfering and other offences'. Employed by James Lumley, a local fish merchant, the errant son had begun to exasperate his father, who had little idea how to handle the boy's increasingly wayward behaviour.

On the afternoon of Thursday, 11 November 1880, a Ballingdon brewer and alehouse owner by the name of Charles Butcher apprehended the young William Bear, who was accused of stealing a purse. Tying a rope around the boy's waist, Butcher interrogated the youngster until he confessed to the theft. Butcher then sent word that he wished to see the boy's father, although it was William's mother who eventually came to retrieve the lad.

The next night, at around ten o'clock, William Bear senior led his son to Sudbury Town Hall with a rope around his neck. Confronted by the desk clerk, Police Sergeant Herbert, the father announced that he wanted his son to be locked up. However, unwilling to take custody of a child under the age of 11, Sergeant Herbert cautioned the child, threatened him with the birch if he appeared before him again and suggested that the silk weaver should, 'take the boy home and correct him' – advice that was to prove both inadvisable and fatal.

Young William was led home, hit around the head and confined to his room. His father knotted a rope around his waist and hoisted him up from the floor, attaching the end of the rope to a peg some six feet off the ground. This kept the lad in a standing position and prevented him from being able to sit down. As if this were not punishment enough, his father then refused to serve him any food during the period of his confinement.

On the Saturday morning, serving only to confirm his view that punishment had indeed been called for, William Bear senior was visited by a Mr Grimwood, the local manager of the gas works in Sudbury. He alleged that young William had been tampering with some of the gas lamps on Melford Road and had come to admonish the boy. We can only guess at his reaction in learning about the treatment being administered to the wayward child.

When the father checked on the condition of his son at around three o'clock that afternoon, he found the boy in the last throes of death. Barely alive, having been hung up without any food or drink for almost seventeen hours, the youngster had slipped from his standing position and fallen in such a way as to strangle himself. His father released him from the rope but the lad then appeared to go into a fit. While the local doctor was then called, he could do nothing to revive him.

The coroner's inquest which followed was a protracted affair, provoking strong reactions from the local population. Mr Lynch, the surgeon who presented evidence on the condition of the body, confirmed that the death had been caused by strangulation, not from suicide. The jury returned a verdict of death by manslaughter and William Bear was arrested and taken into custody.

The funeral of the young lad took place on the afternoon of Wednesday, 17 November, at St Peter's Church on Market Hill in the centre of Sudbury. There was considerable agitation among the assembled crowd when William Bear appeared under police escort. He had been carried to the funeral in a horse-drawn cab amid the hollering of the onlookers. The burial took place in the town's cemetery, the large crowd following the procession to the grave and a number of individuals conveying to the vicar their thoughts about what should be done to the abusive father. Local press reports afterwards confirmed that feelings against the silk weaver were 'running high' in the town.

At a special sitting of the local magistrates on Tuesday, 7 December, Bear was charged with the manslaughter of his son and remanded to appear at the next assizes. He was eventually brought to trial in February 1881. The jury was told that while he was not accused of wilfully causing the death of his son, it was up to them to decide if the punishment he had administered had been excessive. In the event, the jury found Bear 'guilty' but made a recommendation for mercy on the grounds

St Peter's Church, Sudbury, where the funeral of William Bear took place on the afternoon of Wednesday, 17 November 1880. The statue in the foreground is of Thomas Gainsborough, the English landscape painter, who was born in the town in 1727.

that there were mitigating circumstances. The young lad was described as 'accidently killed'. In addressing the guilty man, the trial judge pointedly reflected on the nature of the crime and the context in which it had occurred, saying, 'I am told that it has been a common practice in the place where you live to punish children by tying them up. The sooner that is discontinued the better for all.'

Bear was sentenced to nine months in prison with hard labour. He went on to serve seven months, having already been held in custody for the period leading to the trial. On his release, he returned to Sudbury and resumed his life, being recorded in the 1901 census as a 54-year-old 'silk weaver'.

The widespread misuse of children in the workplaces of the Industrial Revolution and the frequent examples of 'melancholy accidents' befalling under-age workers throughout the nineteenth century would eventually prompt new legislation aimed at protecting young people. Despite this, many children still faced considerable hardships and neglect in their own homes, and the cruelty illustrated in the cases of William Bear and Mary Ann Smith may well have been more common in nineteenth-century Suffolk than we care to imagine.

CHAPTER 12

One Drink Too Many

(1885)

*Saunders placed his left arm under her chin and held her, while he
drew the knife in his right hand across her exposed throat . . .*

Suffolk has always been a comparatively tranquil and
safe place to live. For generations it has maintained
a reputation as a sleepy rural backwater, when
compared to other more densely populated counties.
But the nature of rural life has at times produced its own trans-
gressions and tragedies – the deaths and murders that have
resulted from bigotry, jealousy, fear and crime. And, as
elsewhere, it has seen countless fatalities resulting from simple
cases of small-mindedness fuelled by the consumption of
alcohol.

The British obsession with drinking is widely recognized,
and Samuel Johnson's oft-quoted remark that 'there is nothing
which has yet been contrived by man, by which so much
happiness is produced as by a good tavern or inn,' has probably
been an irritation to teetotallers and temperance campaigners
for many years. And since the pulling of many a medieval pint,
the link between drinking and moral disintegration has been
firmly engrained in the public consciousness.

As early as 1552, licensing laws were established in England
to regulate 'such abuses and disorders as are had and used in
common alehouses and other places called tippling houses'. The
later Gin Act of 1736, which placed a heavy duty on gin, was
the first real attempt by the authorities to control the popularity
of drinking spirits. The measure was predicated on the view that
as a result of gin drinking, 'great numbers were by its use
rendered unfit for useful labour, debauched in morals and
drawn into all manner of vice and wickedness'.

Oscar Wilde's remark that 'work is the curse of the drinking
classes' was a reversal of the widely held Victorian view that
habitual drunkenness was the cause of poverty among the

working poor. And it was in the period from the 1850s that restrictions on liquor and opening hours came thick and fast, as governments and local authorities called last orders on unregulated drinking and sought to create a stable and sober workforce for the Industrial Revolution.

But the frequent cases of alcohol-induced violence that occurred at this time in Suffolk, as elsewhere, demonstrate clearly that the lawmakers achieved little success in solving 'the drink problem', while most politicians remained unclear about whether the emphasis should be on sorting out the drinkers, sorting out the landlords or sorting out the power of the regulators.

Incidents of violence resulting from drinking in public houses could often lead to unexpected deaths. An example was the murder of a 23-year-old Sudbury man named Burbridge in October 1867. He was set upon by bricklayer William Martin after they were ejected from *The Plough* public house in Sudbury around closing time. The two had quarrelled earlier in the evening. Martin pulled a knife on Burbridge and stabbed him with a heavy thrust, before making off. Burbridge was mortally wounded and was tended by a local doctor. He named his attacker but pleaded, 'Don't hang him.' Martin was later found guilty of murder. He was described as being addicted to drinking and fighting.

A similar example was the death of Joseph Moore in September 1887. A quarrel broke out between Moore and Charles Williams in the *White Horse* public house in Withersfield one night. It was over a long-standing dispute, with Moore being the aggressor. The two drunken labourers were ejected from the pub and the brawl continued out in the street. In a desperate fight between the two, Moore received a blow that sent him to the ground. He was taken to a nearby inn and put to bed. The doctor was called but could do little for him, and within days he passed away. Williams was arrested, but after hearing the evidence, the jury returned a verdict of justifiable homicide.

Sometimes these alcohol-induced brawls concerned hostility towards outsiders. An inquest at Bury Hospital in August 1854 heard how Robert Elsden, a labourer from Horringer, had picked a fight with two German musicians who were in the *Red House Inn* of the village. Having earlier paid them and bought

The White Horse Inn, *Withersfield, where Joseph Moore died after a drunken dispute in September 1887.*

them drinks to play a tune on their accordion, the inebriated Elsden ended up in a brawl with Henry Dickel and Henry Leisher. He came off worse, dying of apoplexy. The two Germans were committed for trial on a charge of manslaughter.

Even innocent country pursuits could sometimes spark unexpected hostility and death when alcohol was involved. In August 1786, a cricket match at Haverhill between farm servants erupted into a quarrel between the two teams. Stephen Boreham and Abraham Goodland stepped up to defend their positions and blows were exchanged between them. As Goodland gained the upper hand, another man named Webb drew a knife and proceeded to stab him in the stomach with such force that the knife struck the victim's backbone. Webb was charged with wilful murder and committed to Chelmsford Gaol.

Then, as now, a significant proportion of the alcohol-related violence occurring in Victorian Suffolk took place on the domestic front, much of it away from the public gaze. Occasionally this domestic violence would result in serious injuries and, periodically, death. One such case was that of

Esther Susanna Saunders, who was murdered by her husband following a drunken quarrel on Christmas Eve 1885.

George Saunders was a 29-year-old fisherman or 'smacksman'. He had been married to Esther for six years and the couple had three children. They lived at Erskine Place, Lowestoft, close to Esther's mother, Mrs Woodrow. Described later as 'a mild looking and slimly built man', Saunders was a heavy drinker and prone to considerable violence when under the influence. It was clear from all the accounts given that theirs had not been a happy marriage.

Esther was an attractive woman, whom neighbours described as quiet and respectable. Her husband appeared to be jealous of the attention she received and entertained the notion that his partner was indulging in all sorts of skulduggery behind his back. Much of this was centred on Esther's friendship with their near neighbours Mrs Mills and Mrs Scales. He accused her of leaving home without his knowledge and conspiring with Mills and Scales to invite men to his house when he was away at sea. Even when he was at home he believed that other men were being entertained in the property and claimed later that he

Engraving of George and Esther Saunders. Lowestoft Journal

had often come home to hear a man running out of the back door of the house, before he could catch him. Most bizarrely, he was convinced that the women had an assortment of pre-arranged signals to indicate whether he was in or out of the house, including hanging things before a window, tapping on the walls or altering the position of the blinds. More significantly, he maintained that Esther was covertly visiting the house of Mrs Scales for 'improper purposes'.

It seems likely that Saunders had been hitting the bottle rather heavily in the lead-up to that particular Christmas. His mother-in-law later testified that he had been a 'bad boy' and had given promises that he would curb his behaviour in the future. He was seen in the street outside his house on the evening of Wednesday, 23 December swearing drunkenly at his wife and pushing her inside the house before slamming the door.

On Christmas Eve, the couple went to visit Esther's mother who was looking after their children. Mrs Woodrow found them to be in good spirits and Saunders appeared to be quite sober. After twenty minutes or so, the couple left, apparently on friendly terms. The time was half past eight.

What happened in the hour following their departure remains unclear, although it seems likely that Saunders found time to consume a quantity of alcohol. At half past nine Esther revisited her mother's house and stayed for a few minutes before announcing that she was heading home. Her return to Erskine Place prompted a quarrel with Saunders – what the neighbours later described as a 'naggling conversation'. He was convinced that she had been to the home of Mrs Scales against his wishes.

Saunders later confessed that the argument with Esther had pushed him to kill her. She was seated in the back room of the house de-stoning some plums when he came up behind her and removed a knife from his pocket. Just before he reached his wife, Saunders paused, claiming later that something had come over him 'to say that it must be done'. Aware of his presence behind her, Esther turned to her husband, convinced that he was going to kiss her to make up for their earlier squabble. But Saunders placed his left arm under her chin and held her, while he drew the knife in his right hand across her exposed throat, severing the neck from ear to ear.

As soon as she felt the knife, Esther screamed 'Mother, murder!' and rose to escape from her attacker. She picked up a garment that was close at hand and pressed this to her throat before heading out of the house in the direction of her mother's home. Responding to the cries of anguish, next-door neighbour Elizabeth Mills came out of her house and followed her friend down the street. At half past ten Mrs Woodrow heard a knock at the door and a scream from her daughter, who was struggling to get in. Esther was bleeding heavily from the gash across her throat.

The injured woman sat down on a couch and asked for water before requesting that her mother take the wedding ring from her finger. She then asked, 'Where are my babes?' When Mrs Woodrow had assured her that the children were safe, Esther clasped her hands in front of her and exclaimed, 'May the Lord have mercy on my soul!' Uttering this a second time, she let out a final breath and passed away before her distressed mother.

George Saunders made no attempt to escape justice. He walked into Lowestoft Police Station and announced that he had cut his wife's throat with a knife, inflicting 'a slight gash'. He claimed not to know why he had done it and gave an incoherent statement about his wife's conduct and association with Mrs Mills and Mrs Scales. He was locked up in the cells, overseen for much of the night by Police Constable Roxby. The officer later testified that Saunders had been heavily drunk and was recovering from the effects of the alcohol.

Later, in the charge of PC Cutting, Saunders gave a more detailed account of the crime, admitting that there had been an argument and describing the knife attack as a 'clean-done job'. He went on to state that if it had not been for the blood on his hands, no one would have known anything about it.

In the light of his confession, the testimonies of those close to Esther and the production of the murder weapon, Saunders was committed for trial at the Ipswich Assizes on Friday, 29 January 1886. As was typical in cases of this type, the solicitor to the Treasury appointed an independent psychiatrist to visit Saunders and assess his state of mind. Dr Henry Charles Bastian, a Fellow of the Royal College of Physicians, twice visited Saunders in his cell at Ipswich Prison and submitted a report of his findings to the Treasury before the trial. He concluded that Saunders was of 'unsound mind' and had for the past year been labouring under 'various delusions'.

In his opening address at the Winter Assizes, Mr Justice Hawkins said he was pleased to announce that of the forty cases awaiting trial, very few of the offences concerned were of a 'serious nature' and a significant proportion involved either night poaching or riot and malicious damage to property. By far the most serious charge was that against George Saunders.

When Saunders entered the dock he was wearing a fisherman's jersey and was reported to be 'composed and attentive'. He appeared to be resigned to his fate and when asked how he wished to plead, replied, unhesitatingly, 'Not guilty'.

Mrs Woodrow was the first witness to be called by the prosecution. Dressed in what the *Lowestoft Journal* described as 'deep mourning', she explained how she had seen her daughter with Saunders on the night of the murder and relayed all the events leading up to the woman's demise. Elizabeth Mills was then called to describe how she had followed Esther to Mrs Woodrow's house and had seen blood flowing from the wound to her throat. She emphasized that there was no truth in the suggestions that she and Esther had acted together to lure men to Erskine Place while George Saunders was away at sea and denied that any signals had been used to broadcast when the fisherman was out of the house.

In her evidence, Mrs Scales said the couple lived happily enough but confirmed that Saunders was noisy and quarrelsome when drunk. She testified to hearing Esther cry out 'Mother, murder!' on the night in question and gave an account of how she watched the injured woman staggering around the corner towards her mother's house, with Elizabeth Mills following.

Three police officers were called to give evidence. PC Florry said that he had had Saunders in his charge for several hours on Christmas Day and described the rambling conversations of the prisoner. He explained that Saunders was 'very excited' and had asked several times if his wife was dead. When told that she was, he cried bitterly and exclaimed, 'Oh! Don't let me see her; put me in the fire; kill me; give me some poison; put me out of my misery; put a rope around my neck and hang me.' He had apparently begged the police officer not to leave him alone.

Acting for the defence, Mr Simms Reeve did not set out to challenge the facts presented by the prosecution and explained that if the jury was satisfied that George Saunders had committed the act, his aim was to prove that the man was of unsound mind at the time of the murder. He stated that there was a history of insanity in the Saunders family, evidenced by the fact that the man's father had committed suicide. He also explained that Dr Bastian's views on the state of Saunders's mind supported the claim that the fisherman had been insane when he took the knife to his wife's throat.

One of the witnesses called to support the theory of insanity was Charles Day, a local fish merchant. He described Saunders's childhood and explained how the boy used to jump off the ground and make a noise like a dog and had generally been a great deal of trouble to his parents. He also said that the family had tried to get him into an institution to help him with his mental state. However, when cross-examined, Day could not name the institution concerned.

When called to give his evidence, Dr Bastian explained that he had considerable experience and had often been employed to examine the sanity of prisoners. He had concluded that Saunders was indeed of unsound mind and delusional.

When Mr Justice Hawkins summed up, he explained that the jury must be mindful of the law laid down in the 1843 McNaughton case – the first famous legal test for insanity. Daniel McNaughton had shot and killed the secretary of the prime minister, believing that the prime minister was conspiring against him. The court acquitted McNaughton 'by reason of insanity', and ruled that he should be placed in a mental institution for the rest of his life. However, when the case caused a public uproar, Queen Victoria ordered the court to develop a stricter test for insanity. The subsequent 'McNaughton rule' became the standard to be applied by a jury in such cases. It created a presumption of sanity unless the defence could prove that, at the time of committing the act, the accused had a defect of reason – from disease of the mind – so as not to know the nature of the act he was committing or, if he did know it, that he did not know what he was doing was wrong.

The jury took forty minutes to return a verdict of 'guilty'

against George Saunders. Clarifying that they had understood fully the implications of the McNaughton rule, the judge then said, 'That is, you find that he did the act, and that he was not at that time insane so as not to know the nature of the act – is that what you mean by your verdict?' The foreman delivered the telling response, 'Yes, my Lord.'

When told he had been convicted of murder and asked if he had anything to say, Saunders gave no response. In his closing remarks, the judge said that the fisherman had acted 'under the influence of jealousy, of unfounded jealousy' before sentencing him to death by hanging.

After Saunders's conviction, a committee was set up to devise a plan for the future maintenance of his three children. A charitable fund was also established and raised a considerable sum of money to provide for them. The committee decided to obtain permission for the children to be admitted to a home for orphans or a local asylum. In doing so, the chairman of the committee wrote to the Governor of Ipswich Prison requesting that he ascertain Saunders's views on the matter.

Responding on Thursday, 4 February 1886, Saunders wrote to the committee, saying:

> *Sir, – In reference to my three poor little children, it is my wish they should be placed in an orphan home or homes, as I know that I have not anyone in my family in a position to take charge of them. I should indeed be grateful if steps could be taken by any kind friends to place them there, which would be a great relief to my mind . . .*

George Saunders was hanged in Ipswich on Tuesday, 16 February 1886. His executioner was James Berry, who was credited with dispatching 131 criminals in eight years, including William Bury, a man suspected by some of being Jack the Ripper.

CHAPTER 13

The Curious Curate

(1887)

*With an open razor concealed in his left hand, the curate reached out
and drew the blade across the throat of the elderly clergyman . . .*

The arrival of the handsome new curate to St Peter's Church in Cretingham during the latter part of 1886 was welcomed by the Reverend William Meymott Farley, his family and parishioners. The 30-year-old Arthur Edward Gilbert-Cooper came with a considerable pedigree: he was the son of a well-connected Church of England vicar and a descendant of two well-established and moneyed families. Ordained into the priesthood and a graduate of Magdalen College, Oxford, Gilbert-Cooper appeared to have an impressive track record and came at the recommendation of the local archdeacon. With his dark hair, moustache and fashionable sideburns, he had more than enough attributes to endear him to the close-knit community he had agreed to serve.

At that time, the small parish of Cretingham had a population of less than 400. The vicarage itself was a square, red brick building, standing some way back from the main road into the village and hidden partially by trees and shrubs. It had been newly built in 1863 when Reverend Farley was appointed vicar.

Farley was an ageing and generously proportioned man, who could be both short-tempered and finicky. With his characteristically long and shaggy white beard, he had an imposing presence and could boast an impressive clerical career. In his younger days he had served a number of high-profile parishes and had even dabbled in politics, being an active campaigner for Gladstone's Liberal Party. Married three times, the 73-year-old vicar had six children, all of whom had left home by the time Gilbert-Cooper arrived.

Reverend Farley had married his third wife, Harriet Louisa Moule, in November 1881. She was then 40 years old and the

St Peter's Church, Cretingham, where Arthur Edward Gilbert-Cooper was curate in 1887.

widow of Lieutenant Colonel William Moule. Active and outgoing, she had taken to her new role with some enthusiasm, involving herself in her husband's pastoral affairs and taking on the running of the house. Living in the vicarage with the couple were Frank Bilney, a 21-year-old valet and groom, and Annie Wightman, who was employed as a domestic maid. Both lived on the second floor of the large vicarage.

Overweight and failing in health, Farley had become increasingly reliant on Frank Bilney, who transported the vicar everywhere he needed to go. But when the cleric suffered a stroke, which tightened his throat and affected his speech, it was suggested to him that he might wish to pay for a curate to assist him in his religious duties. With some reluctance he agreed to this, accepting Archdeacon Groome's choice of candidate.

Arthur Gilbert-Cooper was accommodated at the vicarage and given a bedroom next to that of the Farleys. An interconnecting door between the two rooms was locked on the vicar's side. The curate relished his new job and settled into the relaxed environment of Cretingham with some ease, soon becoming accepted and well liked in the village. In particular, he struck up a friendship with William Emmerson, the parish clerk.

Harriet Farley also took to Arthur, spending time with him and encouraging him in his services. The two were often seen walking together and taking excursions. While this was probably innocent enough, it was sufficient to set tongues wagging in the village at a time when less and less was being seen of Reverend Farley. By September 1887 his poor health had confined him to his bed for much of the time.

How much Reverend Farley knew of Gilbert-Cooper's real past is uncertain but it was clear that he had some knowledge of the curate's colourful medical history. It also seems likely that he had not shared all this intelligence with his wife, who had only been told that Gilbert-Cooper was 'a very worthy, good young man, but a little weak'. This was something of an understatement.

In her comprehensive and compelling book *The Cretingham Murder*, Sheila Hardy provides an excellent account of Gilbert-Cooper's personal history. Much of his childhood had been spent in Madras, India, where his father had accepted a position as vicar. At 7 years of age he had suffered from acute sunstroke and was laid up recovering from this for many weeks afterwards. It was claimed later that this had had a debilitating effect on his mental health.

Following school and university, Gilbert-Cooper was ordained and began his working life in 1875 as a teacher at a school in Godalming, Surrey. However, his tenure was to last only a short time as he received instant dismissal for making an unexpected and violent assault on one of his pupils. For the next couple of years he took on a number of temporary curacies before becoming ill and being treated for mental illness in 1878. At first he entered a private nursing home but was later moved by his father to Northumberland House in London, which specialized in treating nervous and mental diseases. Failing to respond to the treatment offered, and claiming that he was being poisoned, Gilbert-Cooper made an unprovoked attack on a fellow inmate. Having picked up a dummy knife, he held the man firmly and drew the implement across the inmate's exposed throat. It was a chilling preview of what was to come.

On Saturday, 3 November 1878, the wayward curate was admitted to the asylum at St Luke's Hospital in London. Diagnosed as suffering from 'Mania' he would spend the next four years being treated there before being released, 'relieved but not cured'. Further, temporary curacies followed until, at the end of September 1886, he accepted the position in Suffolk.

In his early months at Cretingham, Gilbert-Cooper appeared to be calm and settled. While Harriet Farley believed he was over-exerting himself during the exceptionally hot summer of 1887, there appeared to be few other concerns. However, by early September, there were some early warning signs. Harriet began writing to Gilbert-Cooper's mother saying that while he was a positive asset and generally cheery, the curate had his 'little faults and failings' and occasionally seemed anxious. One of his own letters to his parents included the admission that, 'I am all mops and brooms and have been for the last fortnight . . . I am not at all the thing . . . '.

By the end of the month it was clear that his mental health had deteriorated. On Friday, 30 September, Harriet accompanied Gilbert-Cooper on a visit to the home of William Emmerson, whose son was dying. The curate read the last rites to the dying child and the parish clerk expressed satisfaction at his friend's conduct throughout the proceedings. However, when leaving the house, Harriet explained to Emmerson that her companion was not 'right in the head'. It appeared that the curate was not sleeping properly and, concerned that he was unwell and no longer able to cope, Harriet talked to him about getting a temporary curate to replace him. Concerned about his position, Gilbert-Cooper wrote to his father saying, 'I must be careful or I shall be incapacitated from carrying on my work here'.

On Saturday, 1 October 1887, Harriet began to voice her concerns about the curate taking the morning service the next day. She was convinced that a fellow clergyman should be asked to take over instead. When Emmerson called later in the day, she said the same to him and again expressed her uneasiness about Gilbert-Cooper's mental state. Following their evening meal and the reading of family prayers at around nine o'clock that evening, all the inhabitants of the vicarage turned in for the night.

We can never be certain about the true sequence of events that led to the death of Reverend Farley later that night. The official version of what happened relied almost exclusively on the testimony of his wife and, as the case unfolded, it was clear that elements of her story raised important questions and concerns.

According to Harriet Farley's later statement, the curate had knocked on the couple's bedroom door some time around midnight. Roused by the sound, the vicar had called out, 'What is that?' Harriet claimed to have heard a 'rattling noise' outside the room and when she got up and went to unlock the door, found Gilbert-Cooper standing on the landing in his dressing gown with a candlestick in his hand. When she exclaimed, 'Good gracious, what do you want?' he said, 'I want to come in' and made an effort to enter the room. Harriet put a stop to this, and having prevented his entry, shut and re-locked the door, before turning to her husband and declaring, 'Why, he is mad.'

Arthur then apparently announced, 'I want to come in and see the vicar.' Reverend Farley agreed to this and Harriet let the curate in. Gilbert-Cooper made no comment and walked across the room, around the bed and over to where the vicar lay, carrying the candlestick in his right hand. With an open razor concealed in his left hand, the curate reached out and drew the blade across the throat of the elderly clergyman. Farley was heard to say, 'What do you mean? What do you mean?' Gilbert-Cooper merely laughed and turned to walk away from the bed, saying nothing further. Before he could reach the door, Harriet heard her husband announce in a low voice, 'He's cut my throat.'

Harriet maintained that she then followed Gilbert-Cooper to

his room, convinced that he had not cut her husband's throat as she had seen no weapon in his left hand. To make sure, she asked what he had in his hand, to which he replied, 'Nothing'. Spotting a razor case on his dressing table she rushed to pick it up, not knowing if it contained any razors, and admitting later that her only thought had been to prevent him from making use of any sharp implement it did contain. Twice she heard Reverend Farley cry out for Frank Bilney to come to help him. Still seeing nothing to suggest that the younger man had attacked her husband, Harriet returned to her room to find the vicar lying on the floor with blood flowing from his severed neck. Horrified, she ran back to the curate's room and pleaded, 'Come and help me; you don't know what you have done', but Gilbert-Cooper said nothing and made no effort to assist her. She continued shouting and went off to wake her staff.

Frank Bilney heard Harriet's cries at a quarter past twelve. Roused from his bed, the groom came to the room and was told that Reverend Farley was unwell and a doctor was needed immediately. The vicar appeared to have fallen out of bed and was lying face down on the floor. Bilney would later testify that he saw no blood and was convinced that the man was still alive at that point. Passing Gilbert-Cooper's door, he heard 'moaning noises'. He then set off to travel the four miles to Framlingham to get medical assistance, still unaware that his master's throat had been cut.

Reverend Farley had apparently died shortly after Frank left to fetch Dr Jones, the family surgeon. Annie Wightman the maid was dispatched to get help from the village and returned with two ladies who could attend to the dead body. They found Mrs Farley in a distraught condition.

When the surgeon arrived some time later he was surprised to see that the clergyman's throat had been cut. The wound was over six inches long and had severed both the muscles and jugular vein of the neck, leading him to conclude that loss of blood had caused the death. He asked for the police to be called.

With all the frenetic activity in the house, no one had made any attempt to restrain Gilbert-Cooper; the curate had dressed and left the house before the police arrived. When Police Constable Robert Moore got to the vicarage and found the curate missing, he immediately identified him as the most likely suspect.

However, in his initial search of the bedrooms, he could see no bloodstains on the towel, bowl or washstand in the curate's room to link him to the crime. Nor could he see any razor.

When back-up arrived, PC Moore conducted a more detailed search of the room and uncovered some much-needed evidence. This included what looked like bloodstaining on the left sleeve of the curate's dressing gown and the towel. The officers also found a bloodstained razor below a looking-glass on the dressing table.

Apprehending Gilbert-Cooper proved to be surprisingly easy. At around five o'clock he returned to the house and was let in by a surprised PC Moore. The curate appeared indifferent to what was going on around him and was allowed to return to his room. When William Emmerson arrived about an hour later and tried to speak to his friend, he found him largely uncommunicative and more concerned about the loss of Emmerson's son than the death of Reverend Farley. He gave no explanation for why he had killed his colleague, but did admit that he had contemplated it the previous day. The parish clerk stayed with him until Superintendent Balls arrived at the house to formally arrest Gilbert-Cooper and take him into custody at Framlingham.

On the morning of Monday, 3 October, the curate appeared at the Framlingham Police Court to be read the charge of 'wilful murder'. Throughout the proceedings, he gave every impression that he was unaware of the vicar's death and was remanded in custody for a further three days. After lunch the same day, the coroner's inquest opened at *The Bell* in Cretingham before Mr Cooper Charles Brooke.

The inquest was very well attended and when Gilbert-Cooper appeared before the jury he was dressed in the full regalia of his position. Throughout the inquiry he appeared totally bewildered.

Harriet Farley was the first witness called. Wearing a colourful assembly of flowers in her bonnet and maintaining a cool composure from the start, it was clear that she was determined to present herself as anything other than the grieving, black-clad, Victorian widow. This would not endear her to the press in the days that followed, and from the conduct of the coroner's inquest it was clear that it did little to arouse any sympathy from the twenty-two local men of the jury. Their

A private home that was once The Bell *public house in Cretingham where the coroner's inquest into the death of Reverend Farley took place in October 1887.*

sharp scrutiny proved to be both crass and intrusive, playing to the rumour-mongers of the village that had already begun to devour any hint of scandal or intrigue in the case.

In giving evidence, some important elements of Harriet's version of events appeared to be distinctly different from that presented by the press earlier in the day. We can only speculate that the press version must have been the result of information released by the police, which in turn had been based on the widow's first statement. In particular, she claimed that it was Gilbert-Cooper who had twice repeated the phrase, 'What do you mean?' rather than her husband, and that it was the latter who had laughed afterwards, rather than the curate.

There seemed to be some confusion and mystery about the lighting in the couple's bedroom. When asked if she had a light on when the curate approached the door, Harriet said, 'I could not tell. I have thought since that I must have lighted a candle before I went to the door, but I can't remember.' Mr Juby, the juror who had posed the question, then asked, 'You were not burning a light?' to which she replied 'No.' Pressing her, he continued, 'Did Mr Cooper leave his candle in your room?' 'No,' came the reply, 'he took it away with him.'

Mr Juby clearly had an appetite for wanting to expose some of the more salacious gossip in the village. He asked the widow if Reverend Farley had any cause to dislike the curate. Harriet replied: 'Certainly not, not for sometime past. During the first nine or ten months there was some misunderstanding, but latterly he had been very different.' The source of the earlier friction had apparently been 'some little unpleasantness about money matters'.

Juby continued by saying, 'I presume you know very well your character has been considerably aspersed?' Despite an intervention by the coroner, Harriet answered him directly, saying, 'I don't mind about it. People will talk.' From the exchange that followed, it was clear that there were considerable rumours that some impropriety had taken place between Harriet and Gilbert-Cooper. In seeking to make the position clear, the coroner said: 'As I understand your reply it is this – there has never been any impropriety between yourself and Mr Cooper.' With some indignation, Harriet replied, 'Good gracious, certainly not!'

The baiting of the widow continued with Juby asking Harriet if Reverend Farley had been jealous of her and whether she and the curate had ever kissed. Doing her best to defend what remained of her reputation, Harriet said Farley had 'too much sense' to be jealous and she and Gilbert-Cooper had never kissed. Defiantly she explained that she had treated the curate as a younger brother and as a 'motherly person' had always been 'accustomed to young fellows'.

At the end of this particular exchange, the coroner asked Gilbert-Cooper if he would like to ask any questions of Harriet Farley. The curate responded somewhat pompously: 'No, I don't think so; she seems to have given a very true and explicit account of the important affair.'

When Dr Jones, the local surgeon, was called to give evidence, his testimony raised a further concern about the candlestick supposedly carried by Gilbert-Cooper. He believed the fatal incision had been inflicted by someone holding a razor in their right hand. As Harriet had maintained that the curate had been holding the candlestick in his right hand throughout the murder, this suggested that she had been wrong and that Gilbert-Cooper must have put the candle down or changed hands in slitting the clergyman's throat.

The jury asked about the apparent lack of blood on the bed given the extensive wound to the victim's neck. Dr Jones said that the small amount of staining he had observed on the vicar's pillow and bed sheets led him to believe that the injury had occurred while the vicar was still in bed.

When the police were called to give evidence, PC Moore produced the razor that had been found in Gilbert-Cooper's bedroom. This was confirmed as the murder weapon and was later identified by Frank Bilney as belonging to the curate. The razor case that Harriet had removed from Gilbert-Cooper's room was also produced. She had apparently hidden this in another room after taking the item. The case had been found to contain only one razor, but, oddly enough, the murder weapon did not match this and would not fit in the case. There was no further explanation or discussion about what had happened to the missing razor.

Other witnesses at the inquest provided some insight into Gilbert-Cooper's state of mind at the time of the death. Frank Bilney said that the curate 'used to tear about and seemed very much worried'. William Emmerson gave evidence about the discussions he had had with his friend in the early hours of that Sunday morning, in particular, how Gilbert-Cooper had said that he had contemplated the attack on Farley the day before.

Having heard all the evidence, the jury returned the inevitable verdict of 'wilful murder' against Gilbert-Cooper. When the charge was put to the curate, he replied, somewhat condescendingly, 'Oh, I can only say it was not wilful.' He was committed for trial and led away by his police guards. Outside *The Bell* an agitated mob had assembled, confronting the clergyman with their cries of 'Hang him!'

The Cretingham murder attracted considerable press attention and Gilbert-Cooper's behaviour in the days following the coroner's inquest served only to confirm that he needed medical help. One press report said, 'the poor fellow's mind is completely unhinged', and when his father visited him in his cell, he became extremely agitated and aggressive.

The magistrates' court hearing on Thursday, 6 October 1887 was nothing more than a formality. Gilbert-Cooper pleaded 'not guilty', and the bench heard very similar evidence to that presented at the inquest. In her testimony, Harriet Farley changed her mind once again, and now stated that it was

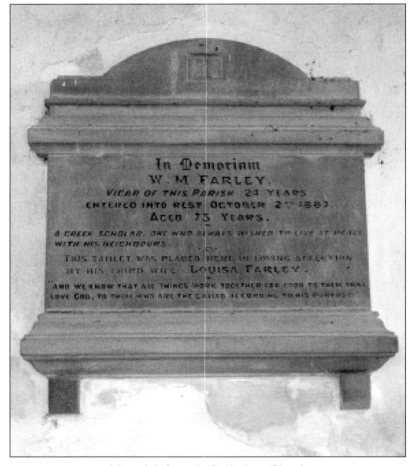

Memorial plaque in Cretingham Church.

her husband who had uttered the phrase, 'What do you mean?' The only new information related to the curate's medical history and the time he had spent being treated in hospital. At the conclusion of the hearing, he was committed for trial at the next assizes.

On the following day the Reverend Farley was finally laid to rest at St Peter's Church in Cretingham. The funeral was both well attended and well reported. Harriet Farley was overcome with emotion during the service, showing every sign of grief for the second husband she had lost.

Gilbert-Cooper's eventual trial took place in Norwich on Tuesday, 15 November 1887. His defence team made no attempt to challenge the claim that the curate had cut the throat of the Reverend Farley, but sought instead to prove their client's insanity at the time of the murder. If successful, this would prevent a sentence of death being passed upon him.

Before the proceedings commenced, the defence counsel made an application to the judge, asking for the jury to consider whether Gilbert-Cooper was in fact fit to stand trial. This would be determined by consideration of the evidence relating to the curate's mental state. The judge agreed to this and the jury began to hear the medical testimony.

The first witness was George Hetherington, a surgeon at Ipswich Prison, who had spent some time in Gilbert-Cooper's company. He outlined the frailty of the curate's mind, saying that the clergyman often appeared to be incapable of answering straightforward questions and could be angry and apathetic. He also talked about Gilbert-Cooper's bizarre actions when in chapel, where he would stand when others sat and utter inapt remarks.

Dr Eager, a superintendent of the Suffolk County Asylum at Melton, said that he had been appointed by the Home Office to consider the mental state of the accused. He stated that Gilbert-Cooper had admitted to him that 'I felt dazed when I got out of bed. I did not know what I was going to do.' In completing his written medical assessment, Dr Eager had concluded that the curate was 'hopelessly insane and irresponsible'.

Incredibly, having heard such solid medical testimony, the jury determined that Gilbert-Cooper was fit to stand trial. As required by the legal proceedings, another jury was then sworn in to hear the case against the curious curate.

When Arthur Gilbert-Cooper was settled in the dock later that day and asked how he wished to plead, he responded firmly and clearly 'not guilty'. The evidence presented against him followed a similar pattern to that of the earlier hearings. His defence team called witnesses who told the jury about the young man's sunstroke in India, the madness inherent in both sides of his family and his treatment while at St Luke's Hospital. Two of the medical staff from the hospital testified that they had visited the curate while he was in Ipswich Prison. One said that Gilbert-Cooper had admitted to him that 'it was foolish and wicked but I could not help it. I did not mean to kill him . . . I suppose I must have been quite mad.' The weight of the other medical evidence left no doubt about the prisoner's acute mental illness.

Throughout the many hours of the trial, Gilbert-Cooper remained largely impassive and unresponsive to the proceedings. The jury eventually returned with a verdict declaring that the curate was insane when he killed Reverend Farley. The judge explained that this was not the question they had been asked to consider and said that the verdict should be rephrased to say that they found him guilty of murder. The jury agreed to this but wanted it recorded that they believed Gilbert-Cooper had been suffering from insanity and could therefore not be held legally responsible for his actions.

In line with the provisions of the 1884 Criminal Lunatics Act, Gilbert-Cooper was sentenced to be detained at Her Majesty's pleasure in the Broadmoor Criminal Lunatic Asylum at Crowthorne, Berkshire. He had avoided the death penalty but would spend the rest of his days incarcerated within the institution, eventually dying on Tuesday, 19 April 1927.

CHAPTER 14

Hardly Worth His Salt

(1892)

. . . holding a pair of curling irons in his left hand, the point of which extended some two inches beyond his knuckles, McCabe struck Francis in his right eye with a single, devastating blow . . .

For much of human history, salt has been a precious and coveted commodity. During the Roman Republic, special roads were built to facilitate the transport of sodium chloride to the imperial capital. In fact the price of salt was strictly controlled: decreases were introduced to allow the poorest citizens to consume it in their diet and increases were used to raise money in times of war. At one time Roman soldiers were paid in bags of salt – the word 'salary' is derived from the Latin word *salarium*, or payment in salt. The substance has also been responsible for much human conflict and misery. Venice once fought and won a war with Genoa over salt, and the *gabelle* – a hated French salt tax that was maintained until 1790 – gave rise to wars, invasions and significant shifts in population. It was another dispute over salt, although not on the same scale, that was to have significant repercussions for two railway workers in Suffolk 100 years after this, in the winter of 1890.

John James McCabe moved into his house in Beaconsfield Road, Ipswich, in May 1890. The 23-year-old was married and had one young child. The labourer soon became friendly with his next-door neighbour, 44-year-old William James Francis, known locally as 'Bill'. It is possible that Bill put in a good word for 'Jim' McCabe with his employer, for on 17 November 1890, McCabe began work as a labourer in the goods yard of the Great Eastern Railway (GER) Company. At that time, work with the GER was highly sought after and the steady employment on the railway would have given McCabe a regular weekly wage without the fluctuations in income to be expected from agricultural or seasonal work elsewhere.

*Beaconsfield Road, Ipswich, where Bill Francis and Jim McCabe
once lived as neighbours.*

Bill Francis was married to Emma and had two children, a 4-
year-old lad who lived with them in Beaconsfield Road and an
older son who was away at sea. He was a skilled platelayer
employed in the permanent way department of the GER at
Bramford Station, on the main line between Ipswich and
Stowmarket, and had always 'borne a good character' in the
thirteen years he had worked for the organization.

On Wednesday, 24 December, Francis was sent by Mr
Curtis, the stationmaster, to purchase some salt from a local
supplier for the points at Bramford. He was given 2 shillings to
obtain the salt, which was to be used to stop the points freezing
and sticking in icy weather. Whether the pair had hatched the
plan sometime before is not clear, but Francis and McCabe
conspired to defraud the company. McCabe obtained some salt,
which was kept at the goods yard and sent this by passenger
train to Francis, who pretended he had purchased it. The next
day, Mr Curtis asked Francis for a receipt for the salt. The
platelayer produced a falsified docket signed by an 'A W J
Raphael'. The receipt was then destroyed.

Why this transaction should have aroused suspicion we may never know, but the transport police of the GER were called in to investigate the purchase of the salt. Inspector G D Power interviewed Bill Francis, who came clean about the salt incident and in his subsequent statement made it clear that he and McCabe had split the 2 shillings between them and spent this on drink at the *Barley Mow* public house on Westgate Street in Ipswich.

As a result of the statement and Inspector Power's report, Francis was demoted from his permanent position at Bramford to work on the gang of a ballast train. While this did not involve any loss of pay, the position was not permanent and was subject to the availability of work at the station. McCabe chose to be absent from work while the police conducted their investigations and, as far as the company was concerned, had effectively discharged himself from duty. The police were unable to interview him regarding his role in the salt incident, and no further action was taken since the falsified receipt had been destroyed. Despite this, McCabe came to blame Francis for his loss of work and over time the animosity between the two disgraced men began to grow.

McCabe was out of work for some fourteen weeks and fell in and out of various jobs, his wife struggling to make ends meet. In 1892 he finally secured permanent work as a currier, or leather dresser, at the leather-cutting works of W & A J Turner, in Princes Street. However, he had no intention of letting the matter of the stolen salt rest and continued to verbally assault Francis whenever he had the chance. In the August of that year he came knocking at the door of his erstwhile friend, referred to the theft and was heard to threaten to kill the older man.

A month later, on Saturday, 10 September, McCabe decided to renew his attack. He had been drinking with James Hartley, who worked with him at the Turner tannery. Hartley met him in the *Friar's Head* at lunchtime and the two carried on drinking until a quarter to four. They then headed back to McCabe's house. At some point, still the worse for drink, McCabe walked up to the back door of Francis's house and, knocking hard on the door, shouted, 'Come out here, you bastard, you stole the salt'. Finding that the man was not at home, McCabe staggered off down the yard, striking a rabbit hutch and breaking the cage.

Bramford Road, which joins the top end of Beaconsfield Road. In its day, this was the main route into Ipswich from Bramford and the route back from town taken by Jim McCabe on Saturday, 10 September 1892.

He announced that he would not seek revenge on the rabbit but continued to use threatening language and at one point was heard to ask his wife for a knife.

Concerned for her husband's welfare, Emma Francis went to meet her husband from work to warn him about McCabe's drunken threats. On the way she met Grace Sutton, a friend who lived locally. The two women met Bill as planned and began to walk home with him. However, he left them at the top of Beaconsfield Road, having decided to stop off at the house of Police Constable Hammond on Richmond Road, to alert him to McCabe's antics. Finding that the police officer was not in, Francis headed for home, approaching his property, as he always did, through the back entrance and along a pathway that ran between McCabe's garden and back yard. It was now five o'clock in the afternoon.

McCabe was in his garden and, seeing Francis, cried out, 'Here comes the thief.' As Francis tried to ignore him and walked up his own yard, McCabe called out, 'Who stole the salt?' Francis turned and replied, 'I know I did, but I have suffered for it, and am suffering for it now.' McCabe was not to be outdone and fired back: 'So am I. I have been out of work fourteen weeks,' to which Francis retorted, 'And a good job too.'

As Francis stood at his back door, the incensed McCabe strode up the back yard of his neighbour's property to confront him. Suspecting that a fight was in the offing, Emma Francis came out of the house to intervene and tried to pull her husband indoors. McCabe pushed her aside and gave Bill Francis a back-handed blow. Then, holding a pair of curling irons in his left hand, the point of which extended some two inches beyond his knuckles, McCabe struck Francis in his right eye with a single, devastating blow. The older man was immediately disabled and had to be helped into the house, blood streaming from his face.

James Hartley, who had been in McCabe's garden watching the argument, rushed over and seized McCabe who struggled to break free and continued to shout and threaten Francis at the top of his voice. Inside the house, with the back door firmly locked, the two women tried frantically to staunch the flow of blood with a cloth. They led Francis to the middle room of the house and bandaged his eye, unaware that the blow from McCabe had penetrated the lobe of the injured man's brain.

Grace Sutton was instructed to leave by the front door to fetch PC Hammond. She left Beaconsfield Road without delay but returned a short while later to announce that the police officer was still not in. McCabe was continuing to shout abuse from outside the back of the house and Hartley was still doing his best to restrain him.

At around eight-fifteen that evening, Emma Francis herself called at the house of PC Hammond in Richmond Road. This time he was in and agreed to accompany the anxious woman back to Beaconsfield Road. Entering the house, the police officer found Francis curled up on a sofa in the back room apparently unable to speak.

Dr George Vincent, whose local practice was on the Norwich Road, was called shortly after this, between seven-thirty and eight o'clock. For whatever reason, he was given the impression that there was nothing more serious than a speck of dust in Francis's eye. He therefore agreed to call as soon as he had finished attending to his evening surgery patients and eventually arrived at about nine o'clock. The condition of the patient was by this time very serious.

Vincent found Francis lying on a bed, crouched on his right side. He was dressed and holding both hands over his right eye. Examining him, the doctor found a bruised and lacerated wound on Francis's right upper eyelid. The wound was punctured through the skin to the dorsal cartilage and there was a considerable congestion and haemorrhaging of blood behind the eye. The railway worker was dazed and appeared to be incapable of volunteering a statement, responding only in monosyllables to the questions posed by the doctor. Vincent agreed to visit him again first thing the next morning.

Meanwhile, at around midnight, residents in the Handford Road area of the town were aroused by the drunken antics of Jim McCabe who, while still in the company of James Hartley, had clearly not calmed down. Standing outside the house of William John Reynolds, a clerk at 168 Handford Road, he was heard to shout, 'Come out you bastard, I have done one today and I will serve you the same.'

Dr Vincent visited Beaconsfield Road as planned on the Sunday morning. Francis appeared to be no better – his temperature had risen and his pulse was now slower than before. The doctor arranged to call again later in the day. PC Hammond also stopped by at a quarter to five that afternoon. He found Francis in bed, completely unconscious. Seriously concerned about the man's health, he left to contact the chief constable, who instructed the officer to arrest McCabe as soon as possible. Finding no one at home in the McCabe house when he returned, he stood guard in the passageway of the property intent on apprehending the errant labourer as soon as he put in an appearance.

When Dr Vincent called again at twenty-five minutes past six, he found that Francis was still unconscious but managed to get him to swallow a little milk. Revisiting the house a final time at nine-thirty he recognized that he could do nothing further for the man, who had begun to pass away: by eleven o'clock that night he was pronounced dead. Vincent recorded the cause of death as a fracture of the base of the skull, which must have been caused by considerable violence. He was convinced that a straightforward blow from a man's fist could not have caused the injuries he had observed – the orbital plate above the eyelid was knocked away and the impact of the injury had been upward and outward.

At ten minutes to twelve, McCabe and his wife returned to their house. Stepping out of the passageway, PC Hammond asked McCabe to accompany him to the police station and called another officer over to assist. McCabe agreed to go quietly and surrendered himself to the officers. On their walk back to the station he admitted:

> *I know I struck him and I am sorry for it. I should not have done it, only I had been drinking. We had some words and I lost my temper. I would rather have given a sovereign than have hurt poor old Bill. I hope he is not hurt much. I hope he is not dead.*

The charges against him were read out at the station house. On hearing that he was accused of striking Bill Francis with an

The Bramford Road Schoolroom, where the coroner's inquest into the death of Bill Francis was held in September 1892. It is now the Ipswich Record Office.

'instrument', McCabe announced, 'I did not strike him with any instrument. That I can swear.' PC Hammond's subsequent search of the prisoner's home revealed a pair of curling irons on the mantelpiece in the back room of the house.

McCabe was brought before the local magistrates at the Ipswich Police Court on Monday, 12 September 1892. However, no formal charges were brought against him and the case was adjourned pending the outcome of the coroner's inquest, which was set for later that same day. It opened in the evening, at the Bramford Road schoolroom, before the Ipswich Borough Coroner, H M Jackaman. The foreman of the jury was a Mr H Austin. Mr H K Moseley asked and obtained permission to represent Jim McCabe at the proceedings.

The first task of the jury was to visit the house in Beaconsfield Road to view the body of the deceased. This took only a short time and when the jury returned, the coroner asked Emma Francis to give evidence. However, overcome by her emotions, the widow was unable to testify and she was allowed to stand down. Her friend, Grace Sutton, a 25-year-old machinist from Black Horse Lane, was asked instead to give an account of the events on the afternoon and evening of Saturday, 10 September.

The next witness called was Dr Vincent, who described how he had attended Francis in the hours leading to the man's demise and the conclusions he had reached about the cause of death. Following his testimony, the inquest was adjourned and McCabe was taken away to be kept in police custody for the next two days.

The resumed inquest, on the afternoon of Wednesday, 14 September, first heard evidence from Inspector Power of the GER transport police. He outlined the details of the salt theft and the action taken against Bill Francis. Mrs Francis was examined after this and gave her account of the fatal quarrel with Jim McCabe. She testified that she saw McCabe punch Francis with 'something in his hand', and asked to describe what she thought she had seen, said it looked like 'a pair of curling irons'. Questioned over the disintegrating friendship between the two families, the widow explained that Mrs McCabe still owed her one pound, 9 shillings and 9 pence for washing and told the jury that she had recently threatened her neighbour with legal action over the non-payment of this debt.

When James Hartley was called to give evidence, his description of the events that day differed in key respects from that of the other witnesses. In particular, while he said that he had watched the attack on Bill Francis, he claimed to have seen nothing in McCabe's hand. Nearby neighbours Mr and Mrs Johnson gave evidence about the threats they had heard McCabe shouting that afternoon, as did Susan Beck, another Beaconsfield Road resident. None of these witnesses had seen the assault, however. The inquest was then adjourned for a second time, to allow the results of the post-mortem to be presented.

The third and final sitting of the inquest took place at the town hall in Ipswich at three o'clock on Monday, 19 September. By this time, the case was attracting considerable public and press attention and the galleries were packed to capacity, with large numbers of people gathered outside, unable to gain access.

Dr Vincent was called first to present the results of the post-mortem examination carried out thirty-six hours after the death. He had been assisted by George Elliston, a police surgeon. The detailed results presented did not alter the basic conclusion arrived at earlier, namely that the injuries to Bill Francis could not have been caused by a fist alone.

When the remaining evidence had been heard, the jury retired for an hour and a half. The verdict returned was that the 'Deceased died from inflammation of the brain, caused by a blow from a blunt-pointed instrument, struck by McCabe, without any provocation on the part of the deceased.' The coroner said this amounted to a verdict of murder, but was then challenged by Mr Austin, the foreman, who said that the jury wished the verdict they had written down to be taken. Mr Moseley, representing McCabe, questioned whether the verdict *was* one of murder, given that there was an absence of malice. The coroner replied that the law presumed that to be the case and the jury eventually signed the verdict as one of 'murder'. McCabe gave no reply when asked if he had anything to say in response to the verdict given.

McCabe's appearance before the Ipswich Bench on Friday, 30 September, was nothing more than a formality. The session was chaired by the mayor, Mr C Cowell, and heard similar evidence to that presented at the coroner's inquest. McCabe's defence barrister, Mr Moseley, was again present and said that the earlier verdict of murder was given against the express wish of the coroner's jury and asked the bench to consider whether anything more than a charge of manslaughter could be sustained by the prosecution. Ignoring the plea, the magistrate decided to commit the prisoner for trial at the next assizes on the full charge.

The Winter Assizes of 1892 were held at the Shirehall in Ipswich before Mr Justice Hawkins. McCabe's trial took place on Saturday, 3 December in a session that included a number of other, more minor, cases. Justice Hawkins opened the proceedings at half-past ten that morning and, with only half an hour for lunch, concluded the final case at around midnight.

McCabe was defended by Mr Simms Reeve, who was instructed by Mr Moseley. Mr J P Rawlinson led the team for the prosecution and opened the case by giving a summary of the salt incident that had first fomented the friction between Francis and McCabe. The witnesses called then followed a similar pattern to that of the earlier coroner's inquest and magistrates' court. Of the new evidence heard, James Potter, a resident of Beaconsfield Road, testified to hearing McCabe a month before the stabbing threatening to 'corpse' Francis.

Dr Vincent and George Elliston, the police surgeon, repeated their medical evidence on the probable cause of death. Vincent said the wound seemed to have been caused by a dull-pointed, elongated instrument and suggested that the curling irons could have caused the injuries sustained by Francis. However, under scrutiny, he admitted that something else – such as the end of a tobacco pipe – could equally have had the same effect.

When James Hartley was called to the witness stand, his testimony again appeared to contradict much of the other evidence. This included the remark about stealing the salt, which he claimed was uttered by 'a woman in the next house', not McCabe. He also repeated that, having witnessed the assault, he had seen nothing in his workmate's hand. While admitting that they were both intoxicated, he claimed that he and McCabe had spent the period before the attack peacefully smoking short clay pipes.

The defence counsel focused on the issue of the curling

irons. Mr Simms Reeve said that when examined, the item bore no trace of having been used as suggested and pointed out that they were not an instrument like a knife which could be readily cleaned by sharpening. He put it to the jury that the irons had not been used to strike Francis at all and McCabe had in fact been holding a clay pipe in his hand – an innocent enough item to be holding given that he and Hartley had been smoking together before Bill Francis arrived.

He went on to say that if McCabe had intended only to use his fists, it would be natural for him to have the clay pipe in his hand and, as such, he had not intended murder. Furthermore, it was clear that Francis had 'led McCabe into temptation' and the accused had 'suffered severely for it'. The defence contended that, having been angry about the loss of his job, McCabe had been provoked by Bill Francis, whose words 'acted like a lash', and he had therefore struck the man in the heat of the moment. Simms Reeve asked the jury to consider a verdict of manslaughter if they were not certain that McCabe had intended to do serious injury to his neighbour.

In his summing up, the judge said that if a man inflicted a wound or injury on another man with the intent to do him grievous bodily harm and grievous bodily harm or death had followed as a result, the jury had to find that man guilty of murder.

With this thought ringing in their ears, the jury retired at six o'clock that evening to consider their verdict. They began to return to the courtroom some forty minutes later but a disagreement broke out on the way and they were forced to spend a further ten minutes debating the issue. When the foreman, Mr Alexander Christie, eventually appeared in the box, he said that the jury were in agreement. When asked for the verdict, Christie replied, 'Guilty'. The clerk of the court then asked, 'Of what?' Reading from his prepared paper, the foreman announced, 'Of the intention of doing serious bodily harm, and we recommend the prisoner to mercy, believing that he had no intention to kill.' To the surprise of the judge, he added that the jury had not been able to agree about whether McCabe was guilty of murder. Mr Justice Hawkins made it clear that they must agree and, having retired for a further period of time, the jury returned with a verdict of 'wilful murder', coupled with a strong recommendation for mercy.

McCabe was asked whether there was any reason why judgement should not be passed upon him. He stood up and replied simply that he did not believe justice had been done and said the verdict of the coroner's jury 'was forced'. Justice Hawkins replied that it was 'useless to go into that now' and donned the black cap to pronounce the death sentence on McCabe, indicating that he would immediately forward the jury's recommendation for mercy to the Home Secretary. McCabe, who had remained standing, gave no reply, and was led away by his warders.

From the way that the case had been handled from the coroner's inquest to the trial at the assizes, it was clear that McCabe had not been inaccurate in describing his conviction as 'forced'. It is possible that the Home Secretary took this into account when McCabe's death sentence was later commuted to one of penal servitude. In the final analysis, the terrible and unnecessary stabbing of Bill Francis resulted from a dispute over a few bags of salt – a commodity that has long since lost its status as a prized and desirable possession with the potential to initiate conflicts.

CHAPTER 15

A Question of Insanity

(1900)

*Taking in the full horror of the carnage before her, Mary could
see her mother lying in a pool of blood . . .*

Haverhill, in the west of Suffolk, has been a market
town for almost 1,000 years. Its growth came largely
as a result of the county's
thriving textile industry, and
by the nineteenth century the town had
become a major centre for the production
of drabbet smocks worn by agricultural
workers. One of Haverhill's key textile
businesses was D Gurteen & Sons, a
fustian manufacturer first established
around 1784. This firm, which still exists
today, expanded rapidly from 1856,
creating a new mill plant with thirty-two
steam-driven power looms. With this
injection of capital, the Victorian town
prospered, and by 1900 its population
had doubled to around 4,000, and new
homes, churches, schools and public
buildings had been built to meet the needs
of the growing community.

*Advertisement for a
drabbet smock, one of the
items produced by the
Gurteen Mill where Ellis
Backler was employed.*

Alongside the expansion of its
factory, the Gurteen Mill continued to
employ many local labourers as home
workers. One of these was Ellis Backler,
a 52-year-old hair and silk weaver, who
lived with his family in Keeble's Yard, off
Queens Street. The decision to work from home had not been
Backler's choice, however. While working at the main factory,
the ex-soldier – who was known to be generally quiet but prone
to violent outbursts – had assaulted a workmate with an iron

Early photograph of the High Street, Haverhill. Keeble's Yard, where the Backler family lived, ran off this main thoroughfare.

All that remains of Keeble's Yard today – a faded sign behind a drainpipe.

bar and afterwards threatened to kill him. As he had also thrown a knife at another labourer, Backler's colleagues refused to work with him, and he had no choice but to continue his trade from home.

As a native of Haverhill, Backler had a large number of relatives living in the town, many of whom were also employed in the textile industry. He worked upstairs by day at a loom set up in one of the two tiny bedrooms of the cottage. Alongside a small garret, the property had only two other rooms, both on the ground floor. It was one of four similar cottages in Keeble's Yard, all providing homes for some of the poorest inhabitants of the town. The family had lived there for only a few years, having moved from 26 Mill Road some time after 1891.

Backler's partner of twenty years was Louisa Mizon, a 39-year-old hair weaver and finisher at the mill, who came from Wratting, a small village less than three miles north-east of Haverhill. She was a quiet, hard-working woman, who occasionally quarrelled with Backler and had to put up with his frequent bouts of heavy drinking. While neighbours believed Louisa to be Backler's 'wife', his real wife from earlier years continued to live elsewhere in the town.

The sewing room in the Gurteen Mill, Haverhill, where Louisa Mizon and her daughter Mary were employed.

The couple had nine children, eight of whom lived with them in the tiny cottage. The oldest of these was Mary Mizon, who was 15 and worked at the factory. The youngest children were the two newborn twin girls who had arrived in August 1900. It was not unusual for the families in this area of the town to have large families, and a letter written by a 'perplexed pedestrian' to the *South West Suffolk Echo* on Saturday, 17 March 1900, suggests that the situation was not without its problems:

> *the numerous children, who with hoops, skipping ropes and whip tops, threaten injury to our poor feet and legs and with whip lashes endanger our blessed eyesight. Walking in the High Street is bad enough, but it requires a large amount of courage to venture along Queens Street. Whilst children are leaving school woe betide the traveller who is hurrying to catch a train . . .*

It was clear that the arrival of the twins had added to the friction in the already less than harmonious atmosphere of the cottage. It was not uncommon for Backler to threaten Louisa when he had been drinking on a Saturday night, and while he stopped short of using his fists, the stocky, five foot seven textile worker had a spiteful tongue and would often verbally abuse his long-suffering partner. Only days after their birth, Backler had taken to calling the infants the 'Bishop's Stortford twins', a sarcastic reference to the fact that Louisa had spent a fair amount of time during the previous year visiting their eldest daughter Kate Mizon, who looked after a great-aunt in Bishop's Stortford. He had apparently grown increasingly suspicious about the nature of these trips and often claimed the twins were not his.

What tipped Ellis Backler over the edge and drove him to commit murder on Wednesday, 12 September 1900 remains as unclear now as it did at the time. His was a crime that shocked the local population and stayed in the collective memory of the townsfolk for many years afterwards.

The day itself had begun like many others. Backler rose at five o'clock and went downstairs. Returning almost immediately, he announced to Louisa that he would have another hour's sleep and climbed back into bed. At half past five, Louisa rose and headed downstairs, taking the twins with her. She busied herself lighting the fire, putting the kettle on and making a cup of tea for herself and daughter Mary, who also got up to get ready for work. When the factory whistle blew at six o'clock, Backler roused himself from his slumber and once more came downstairs, this time heading for the back room to wash. Both he and Louisa appeared agreeable enough, and when Mary left for work at the mill shortly afterwards, her mother was feeding the twins with a bottle, one on her arm and the other in a cradle.

When Mary returned to the cottage for her breakfast at about eight-fifteen that morning she found her 4-year-old sister alone, crying in the living room, and distressed that their mother had apparently been upstairs for some time. Heading up the stairs to the back bedroom, Mary could hear no sounds and found her mother's bed unoccupied. When she entered the weaving room she discovered why. Taking in the full horror of the carnage before her, Mary could see her mother lying in a pool of blood on the floor of the room with a baby in each arm. All three had had their throats cut. Some seven feet from Louisa Mizon's head, on the top of an oak chest, lay an open razor.

Reeling with shock, Mary ran next door to the home of the Cracknell family and explained what she had seen. Mr Cracknell called for a doctor and alerted the police. Police Inspector William Smith took charge of the investigation and began by tracking down Ellis Backler. Asking questions locally, he quickly found some witnesses who had seen Backler earlier that morning. Daniel Crummey, whose fruit shop was almost opposite Keeble's Yard, recollected seeing Backler heading from home before eight o'clock. George Basham, a labourer, and Jesse Phyper, a farm bailiff, had seen the textile worker heading out of Haverhill on the Wratting Road. When Inspector Smith apprehended Backler just before midday, he was walking alone on the road to Denston, close to the *Plumbers Arms* public house and some nine miles from Haverhill.

By two o'clock that afternoon Backler was locked up in a cell at Haverhill Police Station. An hour later he faced the Justice of the Peace, Mr F Taylor, and was charged on suspicion of the wilful murder of Louisa Mizon and the twin girls. While he appeared hostile on entering the court, he remained impassive throughout the proceedings.

Early photograph of the Wratting Road, Haverhill. Ellis Backler used this route after committing murder in 1900.

The day after the murders, a coroner's inquiry was conducted at the police station. The coroner, Mr J R Wilson, called various witnesses to the stand, including Mary Mizon. She described the events leading to her discovery of the bodies and talked about her father's behaviour towards her mother, saying at one point that 'he could not use a dog worse'.

Mr Herbert John Hargrave, a master of surgery at Haverhill, who had conducted the post-mortem examination of the victims, outlined his findings. He explained that Louisa Mizon could not have taken her own life. This was based on the evidence: 'the nature of the wound, its direction from right to left, its severity, absence of blood marks from the razor to where the woman lay, the relaxed condition of the body and the position of the children on the body'.

The coroner also called Inspector Smith to give evidence and praised the police officer for the conduct of the investigation. Throughout the proceedings, Backler continued to maintain an air of 'sullen indifference'. The inquiry was then adjourned, pending further investigations.

The funeral of the three victims took place on Saturday, 22 September. They were buried in a churchyard in Haverhill. In the burial register, the age of the twins was recorded as three weeks. No Christian names were shown for the infants.

The coroner's inquiry resumed on Thursday, 27 September. There was little doubt what the outcome would be. Ellis Backler was committed for trial at the Suffolk Assizes in November 1900.

Backler's trial was accompanied by the usual media circus and insatiable public appetite for all the gory details of the crime. The public galleries were packed and large crowds gathered outside the Ipswich courtroom. During the period of the trial, the jury was accommodated in the *Anchor Hotel* under the charge of the bailiff.

Among the many witnesses called was a Mr A J Simpson, a civil engineer and surveyor in Haverhill. Largely for the benefit of the ladies and gentlemen of the jury, most of whom were unlikely ever to have ventured into Keeble's Yard, he produced plans that he had prepared of the Backler cottage. The Mizon family members called to give evidence for the prosecution included Mary, Kate (the eldest daughter who lived in Bishop's Stortford), Longly (aged 13) and Arthur (aged 12). Beatrice Cracknell, who lived next door to the family, was also called, along with the witnesses who had seen Backler after the murder had taken place. The expert witnesses were the local surgeon Mr Hargrave and Dr Stephenson, an analyst to the Home Office, who had examined the blood on the razor and other articles found at the crime scene.

Throughout the course of the trial, Backler repeatedly declared that the twin girls were not his. It also emerged from the evidence given by Mr Hargrave, that the infants had been suffering from jaundice and it was his opinion that they had been close to death.

The defence team recognized that the case against Ellis Backler was very strong and that, if convicted, he was certain to face the death penalty. Even though he had pleaded 'not guilty', witnesses were called to give evidence about Backler's mental instability and it was claimed that there was a history of insanity in the family. The prisoner's sister, Cristiana Baker, claimed that their uncle, William Backler, had tried to commit suicide and had been incarcerated in a lunatic asylum. According to her, a cousin, Delhi Backler, had met a similar fate.

The prosecution challenged these assertions. The surgeon, Herbert Hargrave, who had known both Ellis and Delhi Backler for some years, said he was unaware that either had suffered from any mental health problems. However, when cross-examined he had to acknowledge that if there was a history of insanity in the family or any predisposition that way, heavy drinking would certainly exacerbate the problems and 'might bring deterioration of the brain'.

Dr Brown, a medical officer at Ipswich Prison who had examined Backler a number of times, explained how the prisoner appeared to suffer from paranoid delusions and said that this was 'a very common symptom of insanity'. Under examination, Backler had apparently claimed that the 'governors of the town' had 'urged on the people and boys in the town to make fun of him and laugh and jeer at him'. He explained that this was due to a speech impediment he had sustained as a result of a stroke earlier in his life. Brown went on to explain that, 'among the insane it was common for a man to entertain groundless suspicions of his wife'. As such, he was convinced that the prisoner was of 'unsound mind' but likely to be 'perfectly well aware of what he is doing, whether the nature of his acts is right or wrong'.

Mr Whitwell, a medical superintendent from the Melton Asylum in Suffolk, challenged the opinions given by Dr Brown. He was convinced that any claim of insanity was a deception, adding, 'it is not at all uncommon for any person who had committed a crime of violence to assume a taciturn demeanour'. He said that Backler's actions could be explained by a form of mental aberration that had led to a loss of self-control. Other evidence confirmed Backler's tendency to become violent when agitated or mocked.

The last day of the trial came on Thursday, 8 November 1900. In summing up for the defence, Mr North, admitted 'although there was no doubt whatever that the prisoner committed the deed he was charged with, he was not guilty by reason of his being insane at the time'. The speech was delivered with such intensity that even Backler appeared moved, and was observed to have tears in his eyes.

In his final address, Mr Maldon, for the prosecution, countered the claims of insanity by suggesting that 'the delusions from which the prisoner is said to have suffered were not delusions at all and that Backler at the time he committed the crime knew the difference between right and wrong'. The trial judge concurred, and in his summing up gave the insanity theory no credence, saying that while the prisoner may have had some form of mental disease, it did not appear to have prevented him from knowing right from wrong.

The jury took just twenty minutes to return with a unanimous verdict of 'guilty'. While listening attentively, Backler retained his composure, maintaining an air of 'stolid indifference'. The judge, Mr Justice Bruce, then passed the death penalty.

Backler was returned to Ipswich Prison to await his execution. He had but a short time to wait, for later that month the prison governor, Mr Gorsuch, received a communication from the Home Office saying that the condemned man's sentence would be respited. As punishment he was sent to Broadmoor, certified as a 'criminal lunatic'. He died in Broadmoor on Wednesday, 10 September 1919, having never fully explained why he committed triple murder on that fateful morning nineteen years earlier.

CHAPTER 16

Killed by Gossip
(1914)

The schoolmaster took the intimations and slurs on his character
to heart and on Wednesday, 4 November, having not slept since
receiving the communication, committed suicide . . .

The outbreak of hostilities in the First World War signalled a change in the pace of life for many Suffolk residents. Alongside those who volunteered or were later called up to serve in the armed forces, it was clear from an early stage that the county's civilian population, whether in urban or rural communities, could expect changes and hardships unheard of prior to 1914. Feverish preparations, precautions and defensive provisions replaced the attempt at 'business as usual' in the early months of the war, and any sense of normality had soon disappeared. The Defence of the Realm Act of 1914, extended in 1915 and 1916, led to increased governmental control of individual freedoms covering a wide range of factors from travel and bank holidays to the consumption of alcohol. It also provided a new legal framework to tackle any perceived threats to public safety and the defence of the nation – powers that led, on occasions, to unforeseen tragedies in the towns and villages of the Suffolk landscape.

The growing demands of war were felt at an early stage. Men who were exempt from military service were enlisted into the Volunteers and National Guard to counter the threat of invasion. Many young women took up jobs working on farms or left their villages to work in factories. And there were other perceptible signs that rural life had been disrupted. Military traffic on local roads and railways increased, troops were often billeted in country homes and, in many parts of the county, the thunder and thud of guns on the Western Front could be heard on a regular basis. As food supplies ran short, prices rose and rationing was introduced. All these developments increased the pressure to dig and cultivate more land in agricultural areas like Suffolk.

Civilians were not immune to the reality that they could no longer sit back and leave the war to the military – a realization brought home by the shelling of some east coast towns in late 1914 and the start of air raids in early 1915. Civilians and voluntary groups, keen to contribute to the war effort, handed over mufflers, mittens, hospital bags, bandages, books and cigarettes. And there was a certain irony in the fact that, as men from Suffolk's towns and villages rushed to join up in the early part of the war for service overseas, few could have realized that within a matter of months bombs would be falling on their own homes and airships and aeroplanes would become a familiar sight in the skies above their neighbourhoods.

It was in this climate that the fears and anxieties of some communities reached fever point and led at times to the circulation of unfounded rumours about certain individuals. The fear of foreign spies and 'fifth columnists' led not only to the internment of many thousands of German-born citizens, but prompted a rumour-mill about anyone who had even the most tenuous connection to the enemy power. One of the ill-

Wangford village, where William Smith was schoolmaster for thirty years.

fated targets of this insidious grapevine of gossip was William W Smith, a well-liked and highly regarded schoolmaster, who lived with his family at Wangford.

Smith was born on Wednesday, 23 July 1862 at Drewsteignton in Devon, some thirteen miles from Okehampton. At 20 years of age he left his rural community to attend Culham College in Oxfordshire, an educational establishment run by the Church of England. Having completed his studies, in 1884 he took up the position of schoolmaster at the Henham School in Suffolk, a role he was to occupy for the next thirty years.

He was married to Alma Delina Theophilia Morse, a teacher from Bream in Gloucestershire, the daughter of Edmund and Theophilia Morse. She was the same age as her husband and served as the schoolmistress at Henham. Living in the schoolhouse, which catered for children between the ages of 5 and 14, the couple had three children of their own, daughters Gladys and Evelyn and a son, Ted Alexander Montague Smith. The latter, known to all as Alec, would later become a teacher of foreign languages, a career path which would have serious implications for his family.

There can be little doubt that William Smith and his family were popular in the small community around Wangford. His influence extended beyond his educational role and he took it upon himself to get involved in most village and religious affairs. One of his lasting contributions was to encourage the children to pursue extra-curricula activities outside their schooling. This led to a pioneering system of school gardens in the county and the provision of swimming facilities in the river at Wangford. Within weeks of the outbreak of war, Smith had begun to organize a concert to raise funds for wounded soldiers who were being cared for at the nearby Henham Hall Hospital.

The Smith family did have some connections to Germany, however, though these were innocent enough. In pursuing his interest in travelling and languages before the war, Alec Smith lived for some time in Aachen, a spa city in the North Rhine-Westphalia area of Germany, on the border with Belgium and the Netherlands. While there, he succumbed to an illness and his father travelled to Germany to look after him and accompany him back to England. It was the first and only time that William Smith had left his country of birth.

Class photograph of Henham School.William Smith is in the back row and to his left are the two German girls who came to visit the family before 1914.
East Anglian Magazine

Alec Smith also had a German connection: he learnt to speak German and, not unusually, maintained a circle of friends in the country. Some of these visited the Smith family in England, including two young German women who helped out with the running of the school at Henham during their stay. This was hardly evidence of espionage, but was enough to get local tongues wagging when war with Germany was declared in August 1914.

We may never know who first began to circulate the rumours about the Smith family and why anyone would have wished to speak ill of them. But whether intended or not, the groundless chitchat about their foreign connections soon reached the ears of the authorities as the hostilities with Germany and her allies escalated. Using the powers available under the Defence of the Realm Act, the Chief Constable of the East Suffolk Constabulary, Captain J G Mayne, wrote to William Smith on 31 October 1914 with an order requesting that he and his family leave the area immediately. Part of the typewritten notice read:

Whereby the behaviour of any person is such as to give reasonable grounds for suspecting that he has acted or is acting or is about to act in a manner prejudicial to the public safety or the safety of the realm, the competent naval or military authority may by order direct him to cease to reside in any area (specific in the order) within or in the neighbourhood of a defended harbour or area, and any person to whom an order relates shall within such time specified in the order leave the area specified in the order, having first reported his proposed residence to the competent naval or military authority, and shall not again reside in that area without a permit for the purpose from that authority;

And whereas an order dated 30 October 1914 has been made by the competent authority under the within regulations, you, your wife, and family (if any) are hereby required to cease to reside in the county of Suffolk, or in any proclaimed or prohibited area, and to report your departure to the police before you leave and your arrival to the police at the place to which you go . . .

We can scarcely begin to imagine the shock and disbelief that must have been experienced by William Smith when he read the letter on Monday, 2 November. Having little option but to comply with the requirements of the order, he promptly communicated to the chief constable that the family planned to leave the area on Friday, 6 November.

For the next two days the family reeled from the devastating blow dealt by the order. The schoolmaster took the intimations and slurs on his character to heart and on Wednesday, 4 November, having not slept since receiving the communication, committed suicide. He was found by his wife lying in the hay shed of the stables at the back of their home. His throat had been cut.

Two days later an inquest was held before County Coroner A F Vulliamy. The long and tortuous proceedings were conducted before a jury that seemed incredulous at the suggestion that William Smith was anything but a patriotic and conscientious professional who had contributed much to the local community. One witness, who knew the family well, said of William Smith: 'He was loyal to the country, I will stake my honour.'

Other evidence confirmed just how well regarded the school-master had been in the area. A letter to Lady Stradbroke, written by her husband, Colonel the Earl of Stradbroke, who was away from home with his regiment, was read out. It said simply:

I have just heard with the utmost horror about poor Mr Smith. It is too dreadful to think that his death should have been caused by those who had occasion to be very grateful to him . . . I do not think he can be replaced as an influence for the spiritual and general welfare of the village. I often said of Wangford that great harm was always being done by tittle-tattle. I never thought such a tragedy would be enacted as now has taken place. These males and females (one cannot use the words men and women) who have maligned Smith and set about tales concerning him must know in their own hearts that they are in reality just as much his murderers as if they had drawn the knife across his throat with their cowardly fingers . . .

Other testimony helped to confirm that many of the rumours circulating about the Smith family were either inaccurate or wholly untrue. This included the suggestion that one of William Smith's daughters was married to a German. In her evidence, Alma Smith was able to dispel such hearsay.

The coroner's inquest was adjourned after one day, to resume on Friday, 13 November. In the intervening period, the body of William Smith was laid to rest in the churchyard of St Peter and St Paul's at Wangford. The funeral was well attended and involved the schoolchildren from the two parishes of Henham and Wangford.

The resumed inquest focused on the nature of the allegations made against William Smith. Captain J G Mayne was called to attend, but before giving evidence stated that he could not divulge:

information as to the nature or substance of confidential or privileged documents, or as to the grounds for the order made by the competent military authority and served on the late Mr Smith by the police to leave temporarily the proclaimed area under the Defence of the Realm Act.

Wangford Church, where William Smith was buried in November 1914.

While this effectively prevented the coroner's jury from understanding fully the reasons for the order made against William Smith, the chief constable did go on to say that the schoolmaster had not been accused of being a German or a spy, adding: 'I believe he was guilty only of injudicious behaviour and utterances. But that would not necessarily justify the withdrawal of the order, having regard to the special times in which we live and to all the circumstances.'

Having heard all the evidence, the verdict of the coroner's jury was that 'the deceased committed suicide whilst of unsound mind, caused by false reports against his patriotism'.

The heartbreak of the Smith family was not to end there, however. Following the inquest, Alma Smith travelled to Devon to be comforted by relatives. She returned to Suffolk in early 1915, accompanied by her son Alec, who had recently returned from Guatemala in Central America. The pair spent the night in the Henham schoolhouse on Friday, 22 January. Alec arose the next morning and made his way to Blythburgh to fetch their luggage. When he returned to the schoolhouse later that day he found all the doors locked and, forcing his way in, discovered to his horror that his grief-stricken mother had hanged herself. An inquest was held three days later at *The Swan* in Wangford, chaired once again by the county coroner.

Then, as now, it was not uncommon for the rural nature of the county to produce insular communities with their own particular customs. And while much of this created some of the more appealing characteristics of country life, it could, on occasions, lead to both a narrow-mindedness and intolerance towards outsiders that was every bit as damaging as the events being played out on the world stage at that time. William and Alma Smith suffered not at the hands of an enemy power but as a result of the tittle-tattle peddled by their own community. In effect, they were killed by the gossip that so rapidly overwhelmed them.

CHAPTER 17

For the Love of Nora

(1929)

*Unable to comprehend the bloodbath before him, he turned
and left the kitchen with some haste . . .*

Geoge Newton Morley had an exemplary military
record. Serving in the First World War he had been
wounded three times, mentioned twice in
dispatches and decorated with the Military Medal.
As sergeant-major he joined the Army Service Corps in the
period after the war, serving in India until October 1928,
when he returned to civilian life. Accepting a job as a
gamekeeper for a Mr Ryder, the 36-year-old bachelor settled
into a cosy and peaceful existence in the picturesque village of
Cavendish. It was here that he met and fell in love with Nora
Plumb, a woman who would determine his ultimate destiny.

Morley first met Nora in the taproom of the *Bull Hotel* in
Cavendish where she had worked as a part-time barmaid
since leaving school. The good-looking girl, then 25 years old,
from the nearby village of Pentlow lived with her mother, who
relied on the wages that Nora brought in from her bar work
and some domestic cleaning duties. Living with them was
Nora's own daughter, a 3-year-old called Rosie, who was the
result of her affair with Alfred Hughes, at that time the
landlord of the *White Horse* public house in Hundon, some
eight miles from Pentlow. Their romance had been short lived
and when he lost his job and was unable to find work in the
area, Hughes took up a position in Islington, London. He
visited Nora and Rosie whenever he could and wrote often.

George Morley's arrival on the scene complicated matters
for the love-torn Nora. Still carrying something of a flame for
Hughes, the barmaid warmed to the military man's manner and
soon became attached to the quiet and respected gamekeeper.
In the absence of Hughes, she took to seeing Morley on a
regular basis, during which time he proposed marriage to her

The picturesque village of Cavendish, where George Morley and Nora Plumb became lovers.

and announced his intentions to others in the village. Flattered, she was nevertheless uncertain about where her feelings lay, and for some time proved unable to give him an answer one way or the other. Fearing that he might lose her and apprehensive about Hughes's impending return to the area, Morley grew increasingly frustrated with Nora's indecisiveness.

Driven to despair in his love for the young woman, Morley began to make veiled threats about what he might do if she would not agree to marry him. On Thursday, 5 September 1929, his threats became a reality. By eleven-thirty that morning he was seen waiting outside the hotel, watching for Nora, and in the late afternoon took only light refreshments. A little later, during the break between her shifts, Nora emerged from the premises and announced her intention to cycle the three miles to nearby Clare. She asked Morley if he would like to accompany her, but the gamekeeper declined and took to the bar to await her return.

When Nora returned, Morley was standing in the bar

The Bull Inn, *Cavendish, which was originally the* Bull Hotel, *where Morley and Plumb died in September 1929.*

drinking. The landlord's daughter, Beryl Richardson, saw the two exchanging words in the kitchen at around seven o'clock that evening. After closing-time, Nora was again confronted by Morley in the kitchen of the hotel. When Beryl walked in on them, Morley asked her to leave and said that he wanted to speak to Nora alone. Leaving the two, Beryl joined her parents for supper, little realizing that no one would see either of them alive again.

It was almost eleven o'clock when landlord Harry Richardson entered the hotel kitchen later that night. Unable to comprehend the bloodbath before him, he turned and left the kitchen with some haste. He had only to run across the road to reach the nearby police house, and when greeted by Police Constable Talbot, Richardson could only splutter, 'For God's sake come, he has shot her.'

The two returned to a scene of unfathomable carnage. With her feet under the main kitchen table, Nora's body lay outstretched on the floor, her hand still clasped to an acetylene lamp from which leaking gas was continuing to seep. Her face and most of her skull had been blown away by the blast from a shotgun. Across the floor, walls and ceiling of the room were splattered blood and brain tissue.

Less than six feet away they found the twitching body of George Morley – the top part of his skull had also been shot away. He had Harry Richardson's shotgun positioned between his knees. PC Talbot was out of his depth in knowing how to handle the crime scene and called Inspector Hammond and PC Kinsey from the police station at Kersey. They arrived later that night, accompanied by Dr Ritchie, a local surgeon. He pronounced both adults dead and proceeded to record the condition of the bodies. When all the forensic evidence had been gathered and a number of measurements taken, both bodies were carried outside and laid together in a locked outbuilding.

The coroner's inquest into the deaths was held at the *Bull Hotel* two days later, on Saturday, 7 September. It was chaired by Mr T Wilson, a coroner from Bury St Edmunds. Attention was given to Morley's unblemished military record and his standing within the village community. The jury heard that the two had been lovers and that marriage had been proposed. But as Nora had been unable to give him a clear-cut answer, Morley had taken matters into his own hands. On the day in question he had watched Nora, having been told that Alfred Hughes had arrived back from London. All of the evidence pointed to the same conclusion, and the eventual verdict of the jury was that 'Nora Plumb was wilfully shot by Morley, who then took his own life'.

Morley was buried the same day, the coffin being carried through Cavendish immediately after the close of the coroner's inquest. His passing was marked by Morley's two brothers and a couple of regimental friends who had served with him on the Western Front. The crowd of onlookers watched in silence as the grieving brothers paid their last respects to the dead man.

Nora's funeral took place on the following Monday at the church of St Gregory and St George in Pentlow. The ceremony was well attended and a large number of floral tributes were delivered by her family and friends. One wreath of lilies read, 'In loving memory, Alf,' while a simple posy of garden flowers contained the poignant inscription, 'In deepest sympathy from Rosie and Alf.'

CHAPTER 18

Not the Gun that Killed Him
(1929)
'Mike, he got me this time, Mike, I'm a done'er.'

Poaching, like smuggling, has a long history in Suffolk. It is a crime that has always been reviled by those who uphold the laws of the land, but one that is often dismissed by others as the legitimate right of any country dweller to put food on his table. And while the legal archives are littered with examples of career poachers who continually flouted the established game laws, few can claim to have had the longevity and notoriety of the legendary Whistlecraft brothers from Rickinghall. But, as history shows, their nefarious activities sometimes led to conflict and, on at least one occasion, even death.

As the oldest of the three brothers, George 'Joe' Whistlecraft could boast the longest list of convictions for poaching and theft. This said, John and Herbert Whistlecraft were no strangers to either the police or the local magistrates for their nocturnal activities and confrontations with gamekeepers. Born in Suffolk in 1878, Joe Whistlecraft took to poaching as a child. By the age of 22, while nominally describing his occupation as that of a labourer, Joe had already become a familiar face at the local petty sessions. In January 1900 he was charged with stealing six fowls from a Spencer Symonds at Rickinghall Superior and received two months' hard labour as punishment.

Records from the Ixworth Petty Sessions on Friday, 5 November 1909 demonstrate just how busy the brothers had become since Joe's prison spell nine years earlier. The 26-year-old John Whistlecraft was summoned for trespass in search of game on private land at Wattisfield on 22 October of that year. He was fined 2 shillings and sixpence, with a further 7 shillings and sixpence in costs. Herbert, at 28, was charged with unlawfully killing a pheasant in the grounds of

Redgrave Hall on Monday, 11 October and, declining to pay the fine imposed on him, was committed to prison. He was listed as having eighteen previous convictions. Not to be outdone, Joe Whistlecraft was summoned for trespass in search of game at Cork Wood, Rickinghall Inferior, on Tuesday, 19 October. He faced a heavy fine and one month's hard labour. A total of forty-two previous convictions was recorded against his name. Not content with this, Joe also threatened to kill Arthur Wallace, the rat-catcher who had reported him – a threat that he followed up with a physical assault on the man.

Poaching continued to be a mainstay of Joe's adult life for many years after this. On Thursday, 27 December 1928 his illicit activities brought him into a more serious confrontation with a gamekeeper adversary. While poaching on land owned by a Mr Wilson of Rickinghall, Joe was met face to face by the local gamekeeper, John Bayfield. Raising his gun towards the stunned Bayfield, Whistlecraft threatened, 'Stand still or I'll blow your brains out,' before making for home.

Joe was arrested the next morning and later appeared before magistrates charged with entering land by night for the purpose of taking game. Bayfield repeated his assertion that Whistlecraft had threatened to kill him. Joe claimed he had not even been at the scene. The bench retired before returning to announce that the prisoner would face two months' imprisonment with hard labour.

Only a year later, the Whistlecraft brothers were to face another serious altercation with local gamekeepers, and this time the outcome proved to be fatal. On Sunday, 8 December 1929, Joe and Ernest were poaching in Stubbing's Wood, Botesdale, on land owned by Lord Playfair of Redgrave Hall. Waiting in the north-west corner of the wood were Charles 'Ernie' Cornwell, the gamekeeper, and his assistant, Mike Scott. Both were unarmed. At around four forty-five that afternoon, they heard a shot and decided to investigate. As they ran along a lane on the outside of the woods they heard a second and then a third shot, both much closer than the first. Hearing a fourth shot, this time no further than fifteen yards away, Cornwell shouted and entered the woods in pursuit of the poachers. Scott continued to follow in the lane.

Carrying an electric torch, Cornwell caught up with one of the brothers and flashing the beam of light onto him from a distance of some fifteen feet, called out, 'Hello Joe, I've got you this time!' The poacher, who was later described as being 'short and stout', ran off, closely followed by Cornwell who yelled out, 'Come on Scott, come on.' At this stage, Mike Scott was still running along the outside of the trees, about eight yards from Cornwell. After a fifth and final shot rang out, Scott watched as his gamekeeper colleague stumbled out of the trees towards him and announced, 'Mike, he got me this time, Mike, I'm a done'er.' When asked 'Ernie, are you sure it was Joe?' Cornwell responded with a firm, 'Yes, that was Joe.'

Scott checked his watch. The time was five minutes past five. He managed to support Cornwell until they reached a nearby fence, where he left the gamekeeper to rest while he went off for help. Returning about half an hour later with another colleague, Mike Scott found Ernie Cornwell dead. The forensic examination of his body later revealed that there were eight small shot wounds in the main arteries of Cornwell's heart, with additional wounds to his lungs, face and left hand. The shot had also smashed the torch which he had been carrying, suggesting quite clearly that his assailant had aimed the gun directly at him.

The local police arrested Joe and Ernest Whistlecraft at around seven-thirty that evening, at their home in Water Lane, informing them that a gamekeeper had been shot and Joe's name had been mentioned. Police Inspector Brown noticed that the bottom of Joe's trousers were wet and asked him how long he had been at home. Joe replied, 'I came home at tea time.' The brothers were initially taken to Rickinghall Police Station, but were later transferred to the station at Eye. They appeared before the magistrates charged with murder. A search of their home produced three shotguns, all of which were taken by the police as evidence.

Both brothers were remanded in custody until Monday, 16 December 1929, although it was now clear that the evidence against Ernest Whistlecraft was insufficient to secure any conviction. Appearing at Eye Police Court, Ernest was discharged and Joe was remanded to appear at the same court at a later date. Two further, but unrelated, charges against him for being drunk and disorderly were dropped.

On Friday, 20 December, Joe Whistlecraft appeared once more at Eye Police Court, in front of a large public gallery. Lord Henniker was the chairman of the bench, with a Mr G Paling acting for the prosecution. With no entitlement to legal aid, the poacher served as his own defence.

Mr Paling opened the case by describing the injuries to Charles Cornwell. He had twenty-two shot wounds on the left hand side of his chest covering an area of about five and a half by two and a half inches. There were also shot wounds in his left hand and his face.

The prosecutor then drew attention to a pair of worn brown shoes, which were exhibited in the court. These were the shoes Whistlecraft had been wearing when he was arrested. Mr Paling said that plaster casts of footprints taken by police from the crime scene corresponded with the size and outline of Whistlecraft's shoes. They were 'not very clear footprints, but there was a distinct likeness'. He also pointed out that the distance between the footprints suggested that the assailant had run away from the crime scene. He concluded by saying that an expert was carrying out experiments on a gun found at Whistlecraft's home and his report would need to be presented at a future hearing.

Donald Barnes, a chartered civil engineer who worked for East Suffolk County Council, then produced marked ordnance survey maps showing the scene of the tragedy.

Witnesses were called to try to establish that Joe Whistlecraft had been at the murder scene on the day in question. Kathleen Brundle, aged 10, and her older sister, Mary, who lived at the Council Cottages in Rickinghall Superior, said they saw the prisoner walking along the footpath towards Garden House Lane at around four-fifteen. He was described as wearing a long overcoat. In response to questions from the defendant, both girls admitted that they did not see him with a dog or with anything in his hand.

Mike Scott, a horseman from Burgate, was sworn in and explained how he assisted in game-watching on Lord Playfair's property. He described the events leading to the fatal shooting of Charles Cornwell. On Mr Paling's

Water Lane, Rickinghall, where poacher Joe Whistlecraft once lived.

suggestion, the magistrates then decided to hear Scott's account of Cornwell's final words, accepting this as admissible evidence. Scott then explained how he had asked Cornwell whether he was sure that the person who shot him was Joe Whistlecraft. He repeated Cornwell's dying words that, 'Yes, that was Joe.'

Scott was also able to tell the court that the assailant had run off in the direction of the north side of Stubbing's Wood, in the direction of Botesdale. It was his opinion that the gun fired had been a 4.10 shotgun.

Joe Whistlecraft was quick to challenge Scott's testimony: 'Are you quite sure I was the man who killed Cornwell?' Scott replied honestly, 'I didn't say so. I stated I saw a man.' Whistlecraft continued, 'You are not sure who the man was?' Scott was not to be outflanked: 'I am sure now, by your build.'

William Sparks, a butcher's assistant from Rickinghall Superior, then gave evidence. He claimed to have seen the poacher at between four-twenty and four-thirty as he went for a walk along a footpath leading from Garden House Lane to Botesdale Common. He described him walking at 'a good pace'. Whistlecraft pursued his earlier line of questioning and

Sparks confirmed that he had not seen a dog or a gun.

At the prisoner's request, Mike Scott was then recalled to the stand and asked whether the man he saw had been wearing an overcoat. Scott could only reply that the man he saw had been dressed in dark clothing.

Edward Hook, head gamekeeper on the Redgrave Park Estate, gave evidence that there was no lawful shooting in Stubbing's Wood that afternoon. He described how he and Police Constable Stammers had been talking together close to the woods at the time of the incident and had heard all five shots. He recognized the sound as that of a 4.10 shotgun. PC Stammers went on to describe how some 4.10 cartridges had been found at the crime scene.

The final witness called was Police Inspector Brown. He gave details of the brothers' arrest and the search of the Whistlecraft household, which had produced a 4.10 shotgun. He explained that he had been in the district for seven years and had always known the prisoner as 'Joe'. In cross-examining the police officer, Whistlecraft cheekily asked if the inspector knew anyone else in the county called Joe. At this point Mr Paling asked for an adjournment to enable the expert witness on the gun to be called.

The police court proceedings were reconvened on Thursday, 2 January 1930. The bench heard evidence from a shop assistant in Rickinghall who had sold Whistlecraft some shotgun

Newspaper report on the Whistlecraft case.

Lowestoft Journal

" THAT WAS JOE ! "

Shot Keeper's Last Words As Evidence.

BOTESDALE MURDER CASE

A little girl of ten who appeared as a witness, and the report of the dying words of Charles Cornwell, the Botesdale keeper who was shot and killed on December 8th, were features of the proceedings in Eye Police Court on Friday, when George Whistlecraft (aged 54), a farm labourer, of Rickinghall Inferior, was brought up again charged with the murder of Cornwell.

Lord Henniker was chairman of the Bench, and Mr. G. R. Paling prosecuted, on behalf of the Public Prosecutor.

Whistlecraft was not defended.

Mr. Paling, in opening the case, said Cornwell had 22 shot wounds covering an area of about 3½ inches by 2½ inches, on the left side of his chest, and there were also shot wounds in his left hand and his face. After drawing attention to the worn brown shoes exhibited in Court which Whistlecraft was wearing when he was arrested, Mr. Paling said in a field on the north-west of the wood the police found some foot prints, of which they took plaster casts, and these casts corresponded with the shoes the prisoner was wearing. The footprints were at such a distance from one another as they would be if they were made by a man running away from the wood. They were not very clear footprints, but there was a distinct likeness to the shoes the man was wearing. Mr. Paling concluded by saying that an expert was carrying out experiments with a gun found in Whistlecraft's house, and at the conclusion of that day's hearing he would ask for a remand in order that those experiments might be completed, and the expert's report received.

cartridges. The results of the post-mortem were also presented, as were the plaster casts of footprints, together with some cartridges and pheasant feathers taken from the scene. The key expert witness was a Robert Churchill, called up from Leicester Square in London. As a shotgun and ballistics expert with over twenty years of experience, Churchill had given evidence in numerous other court cases, helping to convict a number of high-profile criminals.

Joe Whistlecraft continued to lack legal representation at the court as there was no provision in law at that time for legal aid in a pre-trial committal hearing. In fact, the issue was being debated in parliament that very year and questions were raised in the House of Commons about the Whistlecraft case, bringing the poacher some national notoriety. In the event, Joe was once again given the opportunity to cross-examine the witnesses himself, and he proved to be both robust and insightful in challenging the testimony of those giving evidence. In particular, he took issue with the views of Robert Churchill on the capabilities of one of the shotguns taken from the Whistlecraft home, saying at one point that, 'He say he is the gun expert and that gun takes a long 4.10 cartridge. I say it don't and I think when I say it don't, [it don't]. I have had that gun in my house and it don't fire a long 4.10.' It would not be the last time that the views of the expert witness would be challenged in the case.

As a result of the court proceedings, Joe was committed for trial at the Suffolk Assizes in Ipswich on Monday, 27 January 1930. On the appointed day, the crowds packed out the court, the spectators eager to watch Whistlecraft's performance in the dock. This time, the poacher had been granted legal aid and his defence lawyer was quick to object to two particular jurors who were subsequently replaced by the trial judge, Mr Justice McCardie. When asked how he wished to plead in relation to the charge against him, Whistlecraft replied, 'Not guilty'. Throughout the rest of the trial he remained impassive.

Much of the evidence offered by the prosecution proved to be telling but inconclusive, covering much the same ground as that presented at the Eye Police Court. The witnesses who had seen Whistlecraft on the day of the murder were called again to testify. Mike Scott gave an emotional account of the fatal shooting but could only describe the man running away as short and stocky. When Mr Cassels, the prosecution lawyer, then sought permission for the dying words of Charles Cornwell to be relayed, the defence counsel objected and Mr Justice McCardie refused to allow the court to hear them. This had been a crucial piece of evidence.

Following an adjournment, Robert Churchill was called by Mr Cassels as an expert witness. He discussed the Belgian 4.10 shotgun that had been presented as the murder weapon and a number of spent and misfired cartridges, which had been found at the crime scene. He explained to the court that he had tested the firearm and examined it in detail, along with the cartridges. Asked about his conclusions, Churchill said that he would have expected the murder weapon 'to have a blunt striker' and confirmed that the cartridges examined had indeed been struck by such a firing pin. But when asked about the nature of the gun presented to the court, he had to concede that it had 'a pointed striker'.

Mr Justice McCardie was quick to see the significance of the testimony and interrupted the proceedings, asking Churchill directly, 'It isn't blunt?' 'No' came the reply. The judge then continued: 'That means that it was not the gun which fired those cartridges?' Churchill had to admit that this was the case and said he could not link the cartridges to the gun in question.

For the prosecution, this was an embarrassing and costly mistake. It appeared that while the police had removed three shotguns from the Whistlecraft home, the wrong firearm had been presented to the court. Having consulted his colleague, Mr Cassels confirmed that he had no further evidence to present. The judge then directed the jury to return a verdict of 'not guilty'. Joe Whistlecraft left the dock with a smile and a cheery salute.

In the aftermath of the trial the defence lawyer made an application for the return of the Whistlecraft shotgun. The judge granted an order for this, adding, somewhat sagely, that it should not be used for poaching. It was a demand that fell on deaf ears in the Whistlecraft household.

Sources

A variety of source materials were used in the research for this book, including a wealth of local newspapers and journals – a list far too long to include here. All illustrations are from my own camera or collection unless otherwise acknowledged in the text. The following books may be of interest to those wishing to read more about some of the stories featured in this compilation:

A Grim Almanac of Suffolk, N Storey, Sutton Publishing, 2004.
Constables of Suffolk: A Brief History of Policing in the County, L Jacobs, Suffolk Constabulary, 1992.
Death Recorded, P Wright, Pawprint Publishing, 2006.
Digging up the Dead, D Burch, Chatto & Windus, 2007.
Smugglers of the Suffolk Coast, L Thompson, Segment Publications, 2003.
Some Suffolk Murders, R Deeks, Glemsford, 1985.
The Cretingham Murder, S M Hardy, Self-published, 1998.
The Nichols Murder, R Halliday, Suffolk Local History Council, undated.

TRUE CRIME FROM WHARNCLIFFE
Foul Deeds and Suspicious Deaths Series

Barking, Dagenham & Chadwell Heath
Barnsley
Bath
Bedford
Birmingham
Black Country
Blackburn and Hyndburn
Bolton
Bradford
Brighton
Bristol
Cambridge
Carlisle
Chesterfield
Colchester
Coventry
Croydon
Derby
Durham
Ealing
Folkestone and Dover
Grimsby
Guernsey
Guildford
Halifax
Hampstead, Holborn and St Pancras
Huddersfield
Hull

Leeds
Leicester
Lewisham and Deptford
Liverpool
London's East End
London's West End
Manchester
Mansfield
More Foul Deeds Birmingham
More Foul Deeds Chesterfield
More Foul Deeds Wakefield
Newcastle
Newport
Norfolk
Northampton
Nottingham
Oxfordshire
Pontefract and Castleford
Portsmouth
Rotherham
Scunthorpe
Southend-on-Sea
Staffordshire and The Potteries
Stratford and South Warwickshire
Tees
Warwickshire
Wigan
York

OTHER TRUE CRIME BOOKS FROM WHARNCLIFFE

The A-Z of London Murders
A-Z of Yorkshire Murders
Black Barnsley
Brighton Crime and Vice 1800-2000
Durham Executions
Essex Murders
Executions & Hangings in Newcastle
   and Morpeth

Norfolk Mayhem and Murder
Norwich Murders
Strangeways Hanged
Unsolved Murders in Victorian and
   Edwardian London
Unsolved Norfolk Murders
Unsolved Yorkshire Murders
Yorkshire's Murderous Women

Please contact us via any of the methods below for more information or a catalogue.
WHARNCLIFFE BOOKS
47 Church Street – Barnsley – South Yorkshire – S70 2AS
Tel: 01226 734555 734222 Fax: 01226 734438
E-mail: enquiries@pen-and-sword.co.uk
Website: www.wharncliffebooks.co.uk

Index